KATE MULVANY: A playwright and actor, Kate's writing credits include *Father O Friendly*, *Derek Drives a Datsun*, *Vaseline Lollies*, *Blood and Bone* (winner of Naked Theatre Company's Write Now! Award), *Naked Ambition*, *Storytime*, *Embalmer! The Musical* (Old Fitzroy Theatre Company) and the musical *Somewhere...* (Railway Street Theatre). Her play *The Danger Age* was developed at the Australian National Playwrights' Conference, shortlisted for the Sydney Theatre Company's Patrick White Award and premiered at Brisbane's La Boite Theatre in 2008. *The Seed* won the 2004 Philip Parsons Award, premiered Downstairs at Belvoir Street by B Sharp, then moved to the upstairs theatre in 2008.

Kate Mulvany as Rose and Martin Vaughan as Brian in the 2007 Mimmam production in Sydney. (Photo: Brett Boardman)

The Seed

Kate Mulvany

Currency Press, Sydney

CURRENCY PLAYS

First published in 2008
by Currency Press Pty Ltd,
PO Box 2287, Strawberry Hills, NSW, 2012, Australia
enquiries@currency.com.au
www.currency.com.au

NATIONAL LIBRARY OF AUSTRALIA CIP DATA

Author:	Mulvany, Kate.
Title:	The seed / author, Kate Mulvany.
Publisher:	Strawberry Hills, N.S.W.: Currency Press, 2008.
ISBN:	9780868198262 (pbk.)
Dewey Number:	A822.4

Publication of this title was assisted
by the Commonwealth Government
through the Australia Council, its arts
funding and advisory body.

Typeset by Dean Nottle for Currency Press.
Printed by Hyde Park Press, Richmond, SA.
Cover design by Laura McLean, Currency Press.
Front cover shows Martin Vaughan as Brian and Kate Mulvany as Rose in
the 2007 Mimmam / B Sharp production. Back cover shows Danny Adcock
as Danny, Kate Mulvany as Rose and Martin Vaughan as Brian in the 2007
Mimmam / B Sharp production. (Photos: Brett Boardman)

Contents

The Making of a Really Great Play

Eamon Flack

I want to tell you how this play came about, because it's a terrific story of Australian playwriting.

When Kate Mulvany was twenty-something, living in Sydney and acting and writing plays, she decided it was time to piece together the story of her family. She began to write a novel.

Kate's from Geraldton on the coast of Western Australia. If you haven't been there you might know a bit about it from reading Tim Winton's novels. It's a long, dry coast. In summertime, weeks can pass with barely a single cloud in the sky. The beaches are often surfless, and the sea can be incredibly calm and clear and somehow seem unusually wide. Instead of a mountainous hinterland you step off the dunes onto baked desert and low, rocky scrubland. Every now and then along the length of the coast, sometimes hundreds of kilometres apart, there's a small seaside town, humble and quiet, though maybe seething underneath. Tim Winton often peoples these towns with squinty-eyed thinkers, churning up inside and peering out at the world for a bit of sense. They're usually fleeing in one direction or another—either setting up a new life on the coast, or gathering up enough old life to get out and begin again somewhere else. There's a lot of solitary looking for peace out on the sea in Winton's work—skimming along in boats, fishing, swimming.

This was the place Kate grew up, and it was the poetic world of her planned novel. She worked away at it for months, struggling to make something from the stories she'd heard as a kid and filling in the gaps from her imagination. She got down pages and pages. But then her laptop was stolen and with it went the novel. All that survived were a few scraps about crayfishing with her dad. She didn't have the heart to reconstruct it, and decided to let it slide. Maybe one day she'd come back to it.

Besides, by then her career as an actor was taking off. Kate's a theatre animal. She was one of a small army of actors and techies who started out at Curtin Uni in Perth doing a bit of everything—writing, directing, acting, rigging lights, building sets, selling tickets. Many of them have come east in the last ten years and they've been a distinctly playful and humble presence in Sydney's theatres, both on stage and backstage.

Kate's stage presence is a mix of brawn, warmth and understated elegance. Her eyes can twinkle (she has a tireless sense of humour) but she also has that vulnerable Winton-esque squint: taking a good hard look at the world outside at the same time as sorting through the mire of thoughts inside. There's a good-humoured roguery about the way she tackles a role. She has an inner musketeer, hands on hips, head thrown back, ready to take on the world. One of the trademark weapons in Kate's stage armoury is a wrinkled nose and a delighted, foghorn scoff at the stupidities of life. She seems to find our Australian capacity for idiocy ridiculous and fascinatingly funny. And underpinning all her work on stage is a palpable sense of goodwill towards humanity, even the idiots.

These qualities have been given plenty of time and space to come alive over ten-odd years of acting and rehearsing, often back-to-back. It's a pretty fantastic education for a playwright, to have Kate's acting career. And she kept writing the whole time—nine produced plays at last count, both professionally and in the indie scene. They include *Embalmer; The Musical*, based on her experiences working in a funeral home in Perth, and *The Danger Age*, a coming-of-age story about life, race and national destiny set in Kalbarri. It was *The Danger Age* which got her shortlisted for the Philip Parsons Young Playwrights Award in 2004.

Philip Parsons was the co-founder of Currency Press back in 1971 and one of Australian drama's great champions. The NSW Ministry for the Arts set up the award after his death in 1993. From 2003 it has been in the hands of Company B's B Sharp program, a curated season of independent theatre in the Downstairs Theatre. B Sharp doubled the prize-money and turned it into a commission. The judging process goes like this: any NSW-based writer under 35 can submit a play that has been produced in the previous year. Company B announces a shortlist from these submissions, and asks the shortlisted writers what they most want to write. The award is given to the most exciting project. So instead of being a prize for an existing work, the Parsons Award requires the winner to write a new play. It's a bit unorthodox but the joy of it is that it funds new work and gives it a home to find its feet.

When Kate got shortlisted she was in country NSW on tour with Chris Hurrell's production for Griffin of Debra Oswald's *Mr Bailey's Minder*. Lyn Wallis, then Director of B Sharp, rang and asked Kate what she'd most like to write for Company B. The brief was to think big, not to be limited by cast size or scale, and get back to Lyn with a pitch and a few sample scenes. She had two weeks. Put on the spot and inspired by the chance to think big (a rare opportunity for Australian playwrights today), Kate's mind drifted back to the abandoned novel. Her friend Nick Enright, one of the great midwives of Australian theatrical talent, had read the surviving scraps about crayfishing and said there was a play in there. At the time Kate was too stung by her loss to take up the idea, but now the moment seemed right. She reworked the passages about crayfishing and sent them off. A few weeks later, David Hare delivered the annual Parsons Lecture at Belvoir St Theatre. It was entitled 'Why Fabulate?' At the end of it he presented Kate with the 2004 Philip Parsons Young Playwright's Award.

So Kate tucked herself away and fabulated a draft. Then, egged on by Company B's Literary Manager, Anthony Weigh, she refabulated. And refabulated and refabulated. Two years later I followed Anthony into the Literary Manager job and Kate sent me Draft Four of *The Seed*.

There's a strange kind of life cycle to a good play that's hard to describe: you want a play to perform for you, you need to be able to imagine it 'doing its thing'. And if it can't find its motion pretty quickly after the writing begins, there's a good chance it never will.

Draft Four had dance. What had begun as an epic spread across decades and continents now took place in a single town in the UK on a single evening with three characters—an Irishman, an Englishman and an Australian. And, yes, it was funny, but it was also terribly moving. We talked it through, Kate did another draft, then three wonderful actors—Danny Adcock (for whom Kate had written the role of Danny), Belinda Bromilow and Tony Phelan—did a reading in front of a small invited audience. The applause at the end was big and heartfelt but it was the talk in the pub that confirmed our hopes: somehow, Kate had turned a troubled work-in-progress about a real family's knotted rope of stories into a genuinely moving new Australian play with a need to be performed.

It still wasn't finished, though. We asked Iain Sinclair to direct it Downstairs as part of the 2007 B Sharp season. Iain has a great ear for new work and is a long-time collaborator of Kate's. He talked her through another few drafts before rehearsals began on the play in mid 2007.

Danny Adcock, who had been such a force as Danny in the reading, went out of his way to stay with *The Seed* in production. Martin Vaughan had played opposite Kate in the original season of *Mr Bailey's Minder* and now she coaxed him out of retirement to play Brian. Iain's most cunning piece of casting was to convince Kate to play Rose. The show opened in the little three-sided Downstairs Theatre at Belvoir St on a simple set, simply lit: an old couch and chair, dull carpet, a statue of Mary on a mantlepiece, and tattered 1970s wallpaper of Sherwood Forest. The performances were a revelation—loving and cruel, pitiless and delicate, and, in the closeup of that space, achingly honest.

The crayfishing story which began it all was still there (and still is). In previous drafts it had been an excerpt of Rose's writing which she read to her father; now recast as the framework of the play itself, it is in a strange way, emotionally or mythically, the real event. Danny's bittersweet moment of peace out on the sea off his adopted homeland with his daughter Rose is his triumph. Her retelling of this moment is her triumph. It's also Kate's. The story of *The Seed* really ends with the play itself.

At interval on opening night, two lifelong, hawk-eyed reviewers of Australian theatre, Katharine Brisbane and John McCallum, were overheard muttering excitedly to each other about a new work arriving on stage so ready for an audience. Katharine, the widow of Philip Parsons and the co-founder of Currency Press, is one of the most astute observers of the last half-century of Australian theatre. Like Kate she's a West Australian. *The Seed* is the first of the Parsons Award commissions to be published by the press Philip and Katharine founded; and also the first to be given a mainstage season. So in hindsight there was a quiet celebration of tradition and renewal at work that night. John McCallum hadn't come to the theatre intending to review the play, but when he saw it he was moved to do so. He wrote in the *Australian*:

> Kate Mulvany's story, her play about her story and her performance in her play are extraordinarily powerful and moving. This is an important work that deserves a long life.

The season that followed was a great success. After one performance later in the run Neil Armfield overheard someone behind him saying, 'Why isn't this on Upstairs?' and Neil thought, why indeed. *The Seed* is now the first B Sharp production to make the move into the Company B mainstage season.

There's been another rewrite of the play since that first season. (The biggest change has been to move two scenes from the pub where the fight happened and the race track into Brian's living room.) So the published edition you're holding has all the blessings a play could want: a long-simmering need to be told, a great writer with a vivid poetic world at her fingertips and a robust sense of the stage in her body, a commissioning fee, a home at a theatre, a loving director and cast, a terrific first production and a second life on the mainstage.

That's the story so far. I haven't said anything about what this play is about, I'd rather let it speak for itself. But it's nice to think of it as very Australian, in spite of the fact it happens in Nottingham. The real backdrop of the play is that great wide sea off the coast of Geraldton where a father and daughter are trying to learn how to talk about their battles and about the way the past is still here. So this is a play for any two or more people—or any family, or any country—who haven't been able to have a really good talk about what's gone on in their past.

Eamon Flack is Artistic Associate of Company B, Sydney.

The Seed was first produced by Mimmam Productions for B Sharp at the Downstairs Belvoir Street Theatre, Sydney, on 19 July 2007, with the following cast:

DANNY	Danny Adcock
ROSE	Kate Mulvany
BRIAN	Martin Vaughan

Director, Iain Sinclair
Set Designer, Micka Agosta
Lighting Designer, Matt Cox

CHARACTERS

DANNY, 55-60, son of Brian, father of Rose
BRIAN, 80, father of Danny, grandfather of Rose
ROSE, 30, daughter of Danny, granddaughter of Brian

SETTING

Present day setting is in Brian's living room in Nottingham, England. It is a hovel. A small, dark, dank room filled with dated furniture and ornaments, photos and junk—and many, many boxes, all taped securely. Other scenes occur at Heathrow Airport, on the footpath outside Brian's house, on a Geraldton crayboat, and on the 1950s streets of Nottingham. Across the back of the wall is a barbed-wire fence.

ACT ONE

The soundscape suggests a boy running for his life, leaping over fences, in front of cars, over rubbish bins. All the time, the panting getting harder and faster and more frightened...

The clatter of a metal fence...

DANNY*'s young English voice calls out...*

DANNY: Fuck off, pig!

> ROSE, *lit, speaks to the audience.*

ROSE: Nottingham. November. 1957.

> *Another clatter.*

DANNY: Fuck!

> *Heavier footsteps continue running, slowing down steadily.*

ROSE: Danny is hanging.

> *Lights up on* DANNY, *hanging in agony from the barbed wire, his hand entangled in the mesh.*

The wire has weaved a violent gash through his hand and around his fingers, that had've just pinched some cigarettes from the store on Smith Street.

> *The running feet of his accoster slow to a heavy stop. A cop. The footsteps stop.*

DANNY: Let me down, you fat bastard.

ROSE: Perhaps not the best choice of words...

DANNY: Come on! I'm fuckin' hangin' here!

ROSE: The blood trickles from Danny's ripped palm and down his arm. The gravel below his dangling feet is getting more speckled every time he wriggles.

> DANNY *wretches, terrified.*

DANNY: Oh, Jesus...

ROSE: The cop treads his heavy way to Danny and places his hands on the boy's waist.

DANNY: Took your fuckin' time, you bastard.

ROSE: But the cop just puts his hand in Danny's pocket and fishes out the stolen cigarettes. He lights one, and indulges in long, luxurious inhalations as Danny twists to see the policeman behind him.

DANNY: You bastard... you fuckin' piece of shite pig... Those were for me mam and da! Get me down, fuck you, get me the fuck *down!*

ROSE: Danny catches sight of the silvery prongs noosed around and through his mangled hand. Waves of nausea weaken him and he begins to act more like the little boy he is...

DANNY: [*sobbing*] Please, sir, let me down. I'm sorry. I'm tru-truly sorry, I won't do it again. They were for me mam, sir, me da, not me. Please, sir, it hurts. The wire, sir, it's... it's clear through me hand...

ROSE: The policeman slowly moves to the hanging Danny. Once again he puts his hands on Danny's waist, but this time suddenly twists him around, the boy now face to face with the leering policeman. The cop exhales the last of his cigarette into Danny's face and smiles with English eyes.

A man's voice speaks. It is BRIAN, entering his Nottingham apartment.

BRIAN: 'Time to come home, hey, Danny Boy?'

DANNY screams.

ROSE: And he tears the boy from the fence.

◆ ◆ ◆ ◆ ◆

SCENE TWO

A young woman, ROSE, and her father, DANNY, stand side by side in an airport.

DANNY: Where are they?

ROSE: Dad, we only landed half an hour ago.

DANNY: I could do it faster. [*Beat.*] Jesus, where are they?

ROSE: Go and sit down. I'll get the baggage.

DANNY: They're too heavy for you. [*Beat.*] Fuck me dead. Where the fuck are they? Fuck.

ROSE: Go and call Mum. Tell her we've arrived safe and sound. She'll
    be worried.

DANNY: All right.

> *Beat. She hands him a phone card.*

What's this?

ROSE: It's an international phone card.

DANNY: When did they invent them?

ROSE: Same week as the wheel.

> *Beat.*

DANNY: We'll call her when we get to your grandda's. [*Beat.*] Where are
    they?

ROSE: Go and get yourself a sandwich. You didn't eat on the plane.

DANNY: Fuckin' spaghetti.

ROSE: Noodles, actually.

DANNY: Wasn't hungry.

ROSE: Are you hungry now?

DANNY: Maybe a bucket of chips.

ROSE: Here.

> *She gives him some Australian money.*

You'll have to go and get it exchanged. Thirty-eight p to the dollar.
Don't let them trick you.

> *Beat.*

DANNY: I'm not hungry.

> *Beat.* ROSE *takes the money back.*

Where are they? We're going to miss the train to Notts.

ROSE: We'll be fine, Dad. I checked all the schedules. Plenty of time.

DANNY: Takes two hours to get there, you know.

ROSE: I know.

DANNY: On the train.

ROSE: Yes.

DANNY: To Nottingham. [*Beat.*] Where are they?! [*Beat.*] Never took
    this long before. Service standards have dropped. So busy looking
    out for terrorists they've forgotten about the simple things. Like
    giving people their fucking bags back at the end of a fucking flight.

> ROSE *gets out her dictaphone.*

ROSE: What are your other memories of the last time you were here, Dad? At Heathrow.

DANNY: What?

ROSE: Expectation, perhaps? Anxiety? Hope.

DANNY: Rose…

ROSE: Is that what you're feeling again now? Now you're back? [*Beat.*] Or maybe you're tapping into something more deep-seeded. Maybe something long forgotten. Maybe…

DANNY: Maybe a cigarette.

ROSE: Maybe some food, Dad.

DANNY: A cigarette. Definitely.

>   *Beat. The lights fade as he leaves. He stops and looks around.*

Fuckin' tourists.

>   ROSE *watches him leave and switches off the dictaphone.*

♦ ♦ ♦ ♦ ♦

SCENE THREE

BRIAN *enters and begins to decorate the house with dismal decorations as he sings an IRA anthem. He hangs up a decoration that says, 'Happy Birthday, Easter and Christmas'. He sets up three party hats and three whiskey glasses.*

As he decorates, ROSE *and* DANNY *stand outside.* DANNY *is edgy. He stands with a cigarette butt, burnt out, in his mouth.* ROSE *is impatient.*

ROSE: Shall we knock?

DANNY: Jesus, did you notice all the Pakis.

ROSE: Dad.

DANNY: Sorry. Did you notice all the Pakistanis.

ROSE: Does it look familiar?

DANNY: I think it's familiar. I'm pretty sure it's familiar.

ROSE: Is this the house?

DANNY: Maybe it's familiar.

ROSE: It is?

DANNY: I think.

ROSE: Yes?

DANNY: Nothing's familiar. Pakis everywhere.

ROSE: Well, this is the address. Let's go in.

DANNY: See the tops of them trees? Sherwood Forest.

ROSE: That's Sherwood Forest?

DANNY: It is.

ROSE: Your backyard in Geraldton is bigger than that.

DANNY: Sherwood Forest.

ROSE: That's where Robin Hood hid with his merry men?

DANNY: It is.

ROSE: Were they dwarves?

DANNY: What?

ROSE: It's tiny!

DANNY: I lost my virginity in there. Many, many, many times. All the Nottingham boys took their girls there.

ROSE: Why?

DANNY: Sleeping in the same bed of leaves as the great man. Robin Hood. He stood up for his class. Robbed from the rich to give to the poor.

ROSE: What happened when the poor became richer than the rich? Did he swap back over? Must've been hard to keep track.

DANNY: It was a noble act.

ROSE: A thief is a thief is a thief, Dad. Such is life.

DANNY: He won the heart of the fair Maid Marion.

ROSE: He wore green tights and hung out with a troupe of 'merry men', one of whom was a priest.

DANNY: Friar.

ROSE: Whatever. The whole thing belongs on a Mardi Gras float. [*Beat.*] I think it's time to go in, Dad.

DANNY: Laid your mother down in there. Amongst the leaves.

ROSE: Dad!

DANNY: I'll tell you another reason you should show respect to Sherwood Forest, Rosey.

ROSE: It's time to go in now.

DANNY: You were conceived in there.

> *Beat.* ROSE *looks at Sherwood Forest.*

> *Inside,* BRIAN *is tidying.*

BRIAN: [*singing*] Come listen to me, you gallants so fair,
>   All you that love mirth for to hear,
>   And I will tell you of a bold outlaw
>   That lived in Nottinghamshire…

Outside…

DANNY: You do know what he's like, don't you?

ROSE: No.

DANNY: You know what I mean. He's… eccentric. [*Beat.*] And he's…
    got a history.

ROSE: So have you.

DANNY: Not like this man. The things he's done.

ROSE: IRA.

DANNY: Aye. [*Beat.*] But he's a good man, your grandda. A good man.

ROSE: So let's see him. Come on.

> *But he does not move.* ROSE *again gets out her dictaphone.*

How do you feel, Dad?

> DANNY *stares at the house.*

How does it feel to come home?

> *He still says nothing.*

You said it's not familiar anymore. You seem a bit lost.

> *Nothing.*

Dad?

> *He glares at her.*

DANNY: Don't talk to me like I'm one of your stories.

ROSE: You are one of my stories, Dad. My most important story.

DANNY: We're not here five minutes and you're already at me.

ROSE: You have to expect questions, Dad. It's what I do.

DANNY: Well, don't expect answers.

ROSE: You do realise I've gone to a lot of trouble to come here, Dad. A
    lot of expense…

DANNY: Expense? You had credit on the fucking airfares, Rose!

> *She clicks the dictaphone off and busies herself with the contents
> of her bag.*

Sorry, duck.

ROSE: It's fine.

DANNY: At least you got something out of that fucking prat.

ROSE: When did you take your tablet last?

DANNY: Perth airport.

ROSE: Me too. It's time for another one.

DANNY: It's only midday.

ROSE: It's time in Australia.

> *She gets two tablets from a jar in her bag. She gives one to her father.*

DANNY: Fucking things. Cheers, duck.

ROSE: Cheers, Dad.

> *They clink the pills together and swallow them, dry.*

DANNY: Don't know why they call them happy pills. Don't make me feel anything, really. More like having-a-lend pills.

> ROSE *smiles at him.*

ROSE: Come here.

> *Her father goes to her. She straightens his collar, smoothes his hair.* DANNY *smoothes her hair then kisses her softly on the forehead. He moves to the doorway of the house.*

Good.

> *They both stand at the doorway of Brian's house.*
>
> *Inside…*

BRIAN: [*singing*] Robin Hood put his horn to his mouth
>> And blew blasts two or three,
>> When four and twenty kinsmen bold
>> Came leaping over the lea…

> *Outside…*

ROSE: Ready?

DANNY: Ready.

♦ ♦ ♦ ♦ ♦

SCENE FOUR

And they are all inside.

BRIAN: Son.

DANNY: Da.

> BRIAN *gives a fierce salute—fist raised high and strong.* DANNY *awkwardly gives an army salute but quickly changes it to the IRA.* BRIAN *spreads his arms wide.*

BRIAN: Son.

DANNY *drops his things and runs to his father, embracing him tightly.*

DANNY: Oh, Da…

The embrace is over.

BRIAN: You're late.

DANNY: Sorry, Da. They lost our luggage at the airport.

BRIAN: Fuckin' Heathrow.

DANNY: Train to Nottingham got held up.

BRIAN: Fuckin' British Rail.

DANNY: Taxi driver didn't know where he was going.

BRIAN: You don't remember how to get to your own home?

DANNY: I do, Da. I told him. He wasn't from around here.

BRIAN: Paki?

DANNY: Ay, Da.

BRIAN: Fuckin' Pakis. Say it, Danny.

DANNY: Fuckin' Pakis, Da.

He gestures to ROSE, *who is taking it all in.*

Our Rose…

BRIAN *looks at* ROSE, *he is suddenly sweet.*

BRIAN: Rosey…

ROSE: Hello, Granddad. It's nice to meet you at last.

BRIAN: I'm glad you've come.

DANNY: Reporter.

ROSE: I *was* a reporter. I'm a writer now. A documentarian.

She discreetly gets out her dictaphone. BRIAN *spots it.*

BRIAN: The fuck is that?

ROSE: It's a dictaphone.

BRIAN: Watch your mouth, girl.

DANNY: It's a tape recorder, Da. She thinks she's doing a story on us.

BRIAN: On us?

ROSE: On Dad. His history. How he came to be…

BRIAN: Be what?

Beat.

ROSE: But please, feel free to offer any information, Granddad. Anything.

BRIAN: Like fuck. Fucking birthday party.

ROSE *keeps recording.*

ROSE: Sorry. Of course.

BRIAN: I invited you both.

ROSE: Of course. Sorry.

She still records.

DANNY: That's why we're here.

He gives ROSE *a look and she switches off the dictaphone.*

Give your grandda a hug, Rose.

ROSE *puts the dictaphone in her pocket and goes to* BRIAN. *He holds her tight and close, stroking her hair.*

BRIAN: Rosey. [*He breathes deeply.*] You smell like your mammar Maisie.

ROSE: Like Grandma?

BRIAN: Mammar.

ROSE: Mammar.

BRIAN: Lavender and powder and cigarettes.

ROSE: I don't smoke, Granddad.

BRIAN: Grandda. Is smell genetic, do you think, Dannyboy? She smells like your ma.

DANNY: Maybe, Da, I don't know.

BRIAN: Too thin, though.

BRIAN *still holds* ROSE *tight. He takes her face in his hands.*

But she's a Maloney through and through. Good Irish stock. Strong legs. Good chest. Nice pair of hips.

He whacks her arse.

Welcome to my house, Granddaughter.

ROSE: Thank you, Granddad.

BRIAN: Grandda. Welcome to Nottingham. God forsaken place, that it is.

ROSE: Lovely to be here.

BRIAN: The rancid, rotten, hairy hole smack bang in the middle of this shitarse of a country.

ROSE: Lovely.

BRIAN: Now grab a drink and put on a fuckin' hat. There!

> *He directs them to their hats and glasses of whiskey. They don't move.*

Come on! Fuckin' birthday party!

> *They grab their drinks and put on their hats.*

BRIAN: Happy birthday, Rose. Happy birthday, Danny.

DANNY: Happy birthday, Da. Happy birthday, Rose.

ROSE: Happy birthday, Dad. Happy birthday, Granddad.

BRIAN: Grandda. Ey-up!

> *And with an 'Ey-up', they drink.*

DANNY: Watch yourself on that, Rose.

ROSE: I'm fine, Dad.

BRIAN: Let her have a birthday drink, Danny.

DANNY: She's not supposed to drink, Da.

BRIAN: Why not? She's a big girl!

DANNY: She's got to take care.

ROSE: She's right here. She's fine.

BRIAN: Not poorly again, is she? Not poorly again, are you, Rosey?

DANNY: She's fine, Da.

ROSE: I'm fine!

> *Beat.*

BRIAN: Does Glenys still enjoy a drink, Danny?

DANNY: Not really, Da.

ROSE: Mum can't even stand the sound of a can opening. Gives her the creeps.

BRIAN: Is that right? Glenys drank when you brought her over here, Dannyboy. When you finally brought her over to meet us. She drank a Guinness with me right where you're sitting, Rosey. You should have a drink in her memory.

> *BRIAN tops up ROSE's empty glass.*

DANNY: She's not dead, Da.

BRIAN: May as well be. Who ever heard of an Australian that doesn't drink?

ROSE: It doesn't agree with her.

> *She casts a glance at DANNY.*

BRIAN: Why did she not come? I invited her too. She came last time you visited, Danny. The only time you visited.

DANNY: She's working, Da. Doesn't like to let anyone down. Besides, she might feel a little left out, being born on a different day to the three of us.

BRIAN: A good woman. Your ma Maisie never liked her, but I always thought she was all right. Your ma Maisie was jealous of her. Beautiful blonde Australian woman taking her beloved Dannyboy away. The names she used to call her.

ROSE: She sends her regards, Granddad.

BRIAN & DANNY: [*together*] Grandda.

ROSE: She says happy birthday.

DANNY: She's a good woman.

ROSE: She sent you this birthday present.

> ROSE *gets out a birthday present—it is tied with a red bow. She gives it* BRIAN, *who takes it, shakes it and discards it.*

BRIAN: Your ma didn't like her.

> *Beat.*

DANNY: Where are the others?

BRIAN: They're on their way. We'll just have to wait.

> *They all drink.*

DANNY: It's good to be home, Da.

> BRIAN *smiles at him strangely.*

BRIAN: Been thirty years since you been home, Danny. Thought we'd lost you for good to that convict colony.

DANNY: Well, I'm home now, Da. I'm home.

BRIAN: Got a lot to catch up on, Dannyboy.

DANNY: Aye, Da. We do.

BRIAN: You too, Rosey.

ROSE: Ready and waiting.

> BRIAN *fills her glass.*

BRIAN: You'll get your story. Ey-up.

DANNY & ROSE: [*together*] Ey-up.

> *They all drink.*

When are the boys coming over, Da?

BRIAN: You got a cigarette, son?

> DANNY *gets out a cigarette and passes it to* BRIAN *who ignores it. Instead he grabs* DANNY*'s hand and peers at it.*

Still got your scar, I see.

DANNY: I do.

BRIAN: Say it, son.

DANNY: Fuckin' English pig.

BRIAN: Fuckin' English pig. Da. [*He turns to* ROSE *sweetly.*] So you don't smoke, Rosey?

ROSE: No.

BRIAN: Good girl. It's not ladylike. I hated it when your mammar smoked. Remember when you got home after getting that scar, Dannyboy?

DANNY: I do, Da.

BRIAN: Could've belted you, couldn't I? Could've throttled your dirty English arse. But I didn't son, did I?

DANNY: No, Da.

BRIAN: In front of your brothers and all. Has he told you how he got that scar, Rosey?

ROSE: Never.

DANNY: A boring story.

BRIAN: Was smoking that got you that scar. What age did you start smoking, Dannyboy?

DANNY: Don't know, Da.

BRIAN: Don't you lie to me, boy. How long you been smoking?

DANNY: Since ten.

BRIAN: You hear that, Rose? Since ten!

ROSE: Time to give it away, I reckon.

BRIAN: I started when I was nine.

ROSE: Nine!

> BRIAN *nods proudly.*

BRIAN: Which store did you use to steal from, son?

DANNY: I never stole them, Da.

BRIAN: Oh! Pinocchi-nose.

> BRIAN *smiles at* ROSE.

DANNY: I stole a few packs. But I always went to confession afterwards.

BRIAN: Which store was it, Danny?

DANNY: Just one on Smith Street, Da.

BRIAN: Which one on Smith Street, son? The one on the left side or the right side?

> DANNY *doesn't answer.*

Jesus, Danny, was it the store on the left or the store on the right? [*Beat.*] Left or right? [*Beat.*] Left or right left or right left or right left or right?

DANNY: The one next to the lace market, Da! That one! The Evans' store, Da!

BRIAN: The Protestant store, son?

> DANNY *nods.*

The one run by English?

DANNY: Well, we are in Nottingham, Da,

BRIAN: You went into that store, Danny?

DANNY: Yes!

BRIAN: And you stole some cigarettes?

DANNY: I did, Da.

BRIAN: Just like your brothers.

DANNY: Aye, Da.

BRIAN: Only they never got caught. [*Beat.*] And that's how he got that scar, Rosey. My Dannyboy. Chased by a pig over a barbed-wire fence. All for some cigarettes. If that didn't make him quit, nothing will. You should put that in your story. At the beginning. It's a nice violent image. Draws people in.

ROSE: It's not quite the story I'm after, Grandda, but I guess it's a start…

BRIAN: And you should write that when that pommy pig brought him home to me, I bandaged his ickle hand and lit him a smoke, just like he wanted. Didn't I, Dannyboy?

DANNY: Was a long time ago, Da. Don't remember.

BRIAN: I did, my little Robin Hood. I did.

> BRIAN *grabs the cigarette from* DANNY *and squashes it in his fist.*

I started when I was nine, Rosey, but I gave it away at sixty. [*He looks pointedly at* DANNY.] Time for you to do the same, Dannyboy. [*He smiles at* ROSE.] Dirty habit.

DANNY: I'll open a window, Da.

> *He gets up to open one.*

BRIAN: Windows are kept shut.

> DANNY *stops dead.* BRIAN *smiles at* ROSE.

How long did the plane trip take from Australia?

ROSE: Twenty-two hours.

BRIAN: Ooooh! Did you sleep?

DANNY & ROSE: [*together*] No.

DANNY: I never sleep. Do you, Da?

BRIAN: What did you do for twenty-two hours, Dannyboy?

DANNY: Read a book. Looked out the window. Made sure the ground wasn't coming too close too quick.

BRIAN: Always with your nose in a fuckin' book. Always staring out the fuckin' window. How do the wings flap?

ROSE: I beg your pardon?

BRIAN: The wings. On the plane.

ROSE: They don't flap.

DANNY: They stay still, Da.

BRIAN: How does it get up in the air if they don't flap?

ROSE: They're made of metal. They don't flap. It's all aerodynamics.

BRIAN: Listen to her, coming on with the big words. Show-off.

DANNY: They don't flap, Da. You know they don't.

BRIAN: Never been on one.

ROSE: You've never been on a plane?

BRIAN: No.

> DANNY *sighs.*

ROSE: So you came to England on a boat.

BRIAN: Never been on a boat.

ROSE: Well then, how…?

DANNY: Another whiskey, Da?

> DANNY *pours himself one.*

BRIAN: Let her ask her questions, Danny.

> DANNY *takes a long swig.*

ROSE: How did you get to England?

BRIAN: I swam.

> *Beat. He looks proud in his party hat.*

ROSE: You swam. From Ireland.

DANNY: He swam. He did.

> DANNY *takes another long drink.*

BRIAN: Dickyphone, Rose.

> *She looks at him blankly.*

Dickyphone!

> *She gets her dictaphone and switches it on.*

I had to keep undercover, Rosey. Had a mission. Was too dangerous for me to catch the boat so I had no choice but to swim.

ROSE: What was your mission?

BRIAN: I had a package to deliver to England.

ROSE: So you swam it over?

BRIAN: I did. And how did I do that, Dannyboy?

DANNY: With one arm, Da.

BRIAN: With one arm. Kept it over my head the whole way.

> *He demonstrates.*

ROSE: Why did you stay here? Why didn't you swim back if you hate England so much?

> BRIAN *looks at* DANNY.

DANNY: Keep your friends close and your enemies closer.

BRIAN: Put that in your story, Rosey.

> ROSE *stares at them.*

Go on! Friends close. Enemies closer.

ROSE: I'll keep it in mind.

BRIAN: Say it, girl!

ROSE: Friends close, enemies closer.

DANNY: He also got Mam pregnant and she threatened to dob him in if he left her.

BRIAN: That's shite, Danny. Oh, Rosey, I loved your mammar, despite the fact she was English. She was a good Catholic woman.

DANNY: Good Catholic? Da, you knocked her up.

BRIAN: Always refused the contraception, your Mammar. A good Catholic.

DANNY: Ay-I-ay.

BRIAN: So I stayed on here in the Midlands, Rosey. Continued my work.

ROSE: Work?

Beat. BRIAN *puts a finger to his lips in a silent 'Shhh' and signals*
ROSE *to switch the dictaphone off. She does.*

BRIAN: I'm eighty today. Can you count to eighty, Rosey?

ROSE: Yes, Grandad. I'm thirty today.

BRIAN: Grandda. And a beautiful young woman, too.

DANNY: She gives the men back in Australia a run for their money, Da.

BRIAN: I'll bet she does, little slut.

ROSE: I beg your pardon?

BRIAN: Count to eighty for me, Rosey.

ROSE: Dad…

DANNY: Go on, sweetheart. Do it for your grandda.

BRIAN: Go on, sweetheart, do it for your grandda.

ROSE: He just called me a slut.

DANNY: Remember what I told you, Rose.

BRIAN: If you're a journalist you should be more than capable of counting
to eighty. If you do, I'll tell you about my work.

Beat. ROSE *decides to go along with it.*

ROSE: One, two, three, four, five, six, seven, eight…

BRIAN: Good girl.

ROSE: This is ridiculous.

DANNY: Keep going, Rose.

BRIAN: On my lap, Rosey-posey.

ROSE: I'm a grown woman. I'm not going to sit on your—

BRIAN: Rose. Lap. Now.

ROSE, *bemused, sits on her grandfather's lap.*

Dannyboy.

DANNY *moves to his father and sits beside him.*

Now, I've got the paper here. [*He reaches beside him to a worn scrapbook and pulls it out.*] Rose, read what that says for me.

ROSE: 'Nottingham. March. 1960.'

BRIAN: Good girl. Dannyboy. Continue.

Beat. DANNY *reads.*

DANNY: 'Reports from the north say that six British soldiers were
injured and four killed in fighting in Belfast late last night…'

BRIAN: Right, stop there, Dannyboy. So that's six injured and four killed.
How many is that, Rose?

ROSE *is stunned.*

DANNY: This was how I learnt to count, duck.

BRIAN: Rose…

ROSE *is silent.* DANNY *leaps in.*

DANNY: It's ten, Da.

BRIAN: Well done. Good man. Keep going, Dannyboy.

DANNY: 'Reports from hospitals put last week's casualties at thirty-seven with nine English confirmed dead.'

BRIAN: So what's thirty-seven plus nine plus the aforementioned ten, Dannyboy?

DANNY: Fifty-six, Da.

BRIAN: That's right. Good boy. Keep reading.

Clockwise from left: Kate Mulvany as Rose, Danny Adcock as Danny and Martin Vaughan as Brian in the 2007 Mimmam production in Sydney. (Photo: Brett Boardman)

DANNY: 'Last month saw sixteen British soldiers injured and another eight the month before.'

BRIAN: So what's sixteen plus eight, Rosey Maloney?

ROSE: Twenty-four.

BRIAN: And what's twenty-four plus the aforementioned fifty-six?

ROSE *is silent.*

Come on…

DANNY: Eighty?

ROSE: Eighty.

BRIAN: Good! Eighty! That's a good number, isn't it? Nice and rounded. That's how old I am today. And that's the reason we live in this cunt of a country. So Da can do his work. That's my work, Rosey. Eighty. Hasn't Da been working hard, Dannyboy? Keeping an eye on things.

DANNY: Yes, Da.

ROSE *gets off* BRIAN*'s lap.*

ROSE: I'm dying to meet the others.

BRIAN: They'll be here soon.

DANNY: Do you see anyone much, Da?

BRIAN: 'Course I do. A nurse comes around every few days to feed me and give me pills.

DANNY: I meant the boys. Do you see them much?

BRIAN: Oh, aye—your brothers also come round every week or so to feed me and give me pills.

He laughs.

DANNY: Ay-I-ay.

ROSE: What?

BRIAN: Had a delivery a few days ago.

DANNY: What are they? Where do you keep them? [*He glances around the room.*] The boxes?

BRIAN *grins.*

Ay-I-ay.

BRIAN: Gotta make a living somehow, Danny.

DANNY: I know that, Da.

BRIAN: Can't all take off to the other side of the world and build roads for a living. Catch catfish.

ROSE: Crayfish.

DANNY: But drugs, Da…

ROSE: Drugs? [*She looks at the boxes.*] Those are drugs?

BRIAN: Investigative journalist, is she? My boys, Rosey.

ROSE: They're drug dealers?

BRIAN: No, they're just a bunch of very merry men. Some days the boxes have cigarettes. Sometimes mobile phones. Pills. Powder. Guns.

ROSE: Guns?

> *Beat. Then* ROSE *heads towards the boxes to inspect them.* BRIAN *stops her sharply.*

BRIAN: You trying to get your family killed, Rosey Maloney? There'll be no touching of the boxes. They're hidden for a reason, you stupid girl. This is a particularly special delivery. That's why they've left them with me. Their da.

> *As he moves away,* ROSE *goes for the boxes again.*

DANNY: Rose! Leave it!

> *She stops again.*

BRIAN: You want to try the wares, Rosey?

> *He pulls a packet of pills from under the cushion of the couch.*

ROSE: No thank you.

BRIAN: You sure? These little blue pearls are their best seller. Trevor will sell this entire pack in one night when he's on the door of the club. Sell them for ten pound each.

DANNY: Ten pound a pack?

BRIAN: No, Danny, ten pound a pill.

ROSE: Ten pound? That's ridiculous.

BRIAN: Trevor only sells the best, Rosey. Comes round every Thursday night before he starts his shift, counts them out, pockets them down his special underpants he got custom-made in Thailand and then off he goes to work.

DANNY: Trevor's a bouncer.

ROSE: Why does he need to do that when he's making ten pound a pill?

BRIAN: So he can hang onto his social security. Plus, working on the door of the biggest club in Nottingham means the business comes straight to him. He doesn't even have to move.

ROSE: What if he gets caught? Surely the police are around all the time. They could frisk him.

BRIAN: Have you seen your Uncle Trevor, Rosey?

ROSE: Never.

BRIAN: You see that trophy up there?

> *She does. A large trophy on the mantelpiece.*

Mr Britain, 1986. Awarded to Trevor Maloney. Nottingham, England.

DANNY: That was years ago. The man's almost sixty now, for God's sake.

BRIAN: He's still a big man, your brother, Danny. And the special stuff he takes to keep him a big man also makes him a little bit aggressive so I don't think any cops will 'frisk' him any time soon. But he's a good boy. You'll see that. He'll be coming round for them soon.

ROSE: So what are they exactly?

BRIAN: Oh, Rosey-posey, these are the happiest little pills in all the world. They make your smile wide and your insides tingle and your belly laugh and your feet dance with one gulp.

DANNY: How do you know that, Da? They're probably just breath mints. Those kids at the nightclub wouldn't know any better.

BRIAN: Try one.

> *He holds out a handful of pills.*

DANNY: I'm not trying no fucking pills that Trevor's had stuffed in his special Thai underpants. Could catch something.

BRIAN: Rosey?

ROSE: No thank you.

BRIAN: You don't take drugs?

ROSE: Not that kind, no. I'm fine within my… I don't need chemicals to… inside me. I don't need drugs to have a good time.

> *Beat.*

BRIAN: All right, then.

> *BRIAN pops one pill. Then another. Then another. Then a handful of pills. There is a moment of shock from ROSE and DANNY as he chews, crunching them.*

ROSE: Granddad! What are you doing? Spit them out!

> *He crunches. DANNY does not move.*

Jesus, Granddad…

> *She runs to him, her panic slowly rising as he refuses to spit them out.*

Spit them out, for God's sake! That's too much! You'll kill yourself.

DANNY *still doesn't move.*

Spit them out! Spit them out! Granddad, that's too much! *Spit them out, Granddad!*

BRIAN *spits them out into her hand.*

BRIAN: *Grandda!*

Beat. BRIAN *and* ROSE *notice* DANNY *is standing very still in the middle of the room, almost in a trance.*

You all right, Dannyboy?

ROSE: Dad?

ROSE *moves slowly to her father, looks at him closely, touches him very gently, then speaks very softly.*

Grandda, Dad's having a whiteout. I'm going to get him some water. Don't touch him.

She leaves. BRIAN *stares at* DANNY. *He does nothing. Then…*

BRIAN: Ey-up, Dannyboy. Don't worry, Da's here.

DANNY *comes to. He looks at his father.*

DANNY: Glenys?

BRIAN: Da, you fuck.

DANNY: Sorry, Da. Da!

BRIAN: You had a white turn, Danny. Don't worry, I looked after you.

DANNY: You have them too, Da?

BRIAN: [*nodding*] A white turn.

DANNY: Where's Rose? You have them too, Da?

BRIAN: I sent her to get you some water. Da's here, Dannyboy, Da's here.

He embraces DANNY*'s head roughly and strokes his hair.* ROSE *enters with the water. She takes her father and sits him down. Despite his embarrassment and assurances he is okay, she checks his skin, his eyes, his face. She gives him the water.*

ROSE: Here, Dad. Drink this.

BRIAN: Good girl, Rose. Drink up, Dannyboy.

ROSE *turns on* BRIAN.

ROSE: What the hell was that, Granddad?

BRIAN: Grandda.

ROSE: Do you know how bad these are for you? You're eighty, for Christ's sake. You don't realise the shit they put in these things.

    BRIAN *chuckles.*

It's not funny, Granddad. Rat poison, animal tranquilisers—that's what ecstasy really is. Trust me.

BRIAN: It's not ecstasy, Rosey. It's Viagra.

ROSE: What?

BRIAN: Viagra. Trevor's best seller. Little blue pearls of tingly happiness.

DANNY: Viagra. [*He chuckles.*] Ay-I-aye.

ROSE: We thought it was… You just made Dad have a turn!

DANNY: Wasn't that, Rosey. Just tired, that's all.

    BRIAN *laughs gleefully.*

BRIAN: Ecstasy! You thought that was ecstasy! No, Rosey… no, no… [*He reaches under the couch for another bag of pills. They are red.*] That's ecstasy.

ROSE: Oh, my God.

DANNY: [*laughing*] Look, Rose! *Real* happy pills!

BRIAN: Help yourself if you want one, Dannyboy.

DANNY: I will, Da. Ta.

ROSE: Dad!

BRIAN: Rose?

ROSE: No!

BRIAN: Try the Viagra, then. They work on women too, Rosey.

ROSE: That's disgusting.

BRIAN: Your fiancé might like some. Charles.

DANNY: Da…

BRIAN: Pop them in his breakfast cereal and you'll see more than the sunrise in the morning.

DANNY: Da…

BRIAN: Why did he not come, Rose? Or are you going be like your Da and wait six years before you bring the love of your life home to meet your family? You'll want to get cracking, Rosey. Your clock hits thirty today. Get that fuckin' ring on your finger.

    Beat.

ROSE: I'm not getting married anymore.

Beat.

DANNY: I told you in the letter, Da. The wedding's off.

BRIAN: Get rid of him, did you, Rosey? [*Beat.*] Never mind, Rosey. Better to have it all go to fuck now than later. Before you have children. My boys were clever, you see. Got out of their marriages before any babbies came along. Less trouble.

DANNY: Me and Glenys have lasted.

BRIAN: Only because they never made apron strings ten thousand miles long. Remember that poem, Dannyboy? The one that used to make your mam laugh?

He performs to DANNY.

> When me prayers wuz poorly said,
> Who tucked me in me little bed
> And tanned me arse till it was red?

DANNY: Mimmam.

BRIAN: Who took me from me cosy cot
> And put me on an ice-cold pot
> And made me pee if I could not?

DANNY: Mimmam.

BRIAN: And when the morning light did come,
> And in me drawers I'd dribbled some,
> Who cleaned up me tiny bum?

DANNY: Mimmam.

BRIAN: Who wuz glad when I wuz glad,
> Who cuddled me when I wuz sad,
> Who smacked me legs when I wuz bad?

DANNY encourages ROSE *to join in.*

ROSE: My mum.

DANNY & BRIAN: [*together*] Mimmam.

BRIAN: Who would me 'air so neatly part,
> And hug me gently to her 'eart,
> Who sometimes squeezed me till I'd fart?

ROSE: [*laughing*] Mimmam.

BRIAN: Who looked at me with eyebrows knit
> And nearly threw a king-sized fit
> When in me Sunday pants I'd shit?

ROSE & DANNY: [*together*] Mimmam.

BRIAN: And when at night her bed did squeak
        And I raised me head to have a peek,
        Who yelled at me to go to sleep?

DANNY: Middad!

They laugh together.

BRIAN: Maisie.

He pours drinks for all.

To Maisie.

ROSE and DANNY raise their glasses.

ROSE & DANNY: [*together*] To Maisie.

BRIAN: You broke her heart. You fucking cunt. [*He drinks and stands up.*] Come on, then. Pub.

Beat. BRIAN starts to put his coat on.

ROSE: I'm not sure if Dad should go to the pub…

DANNY: I'm fine, Rose. Da, we're not going to the pub.

BRIAN: Pub. Now.

DANNY: We just bloody got here, for Christ's sake, Da.

BRIAN: Danny. Now. Pub.

DANNY: What about the boys?

BRIAN: In time. Pub.

DANNY: I tell you, Da. I'm not going into that fucking place. Rose is tired.

Beat. BRIAN smiles at DANNY.

BRIAN: Scared of something, Dannyboy?

As DANNY and BRIAN face off, there is a shift in lighting and sound and ROSE is on her own. Water laps, seagulls call, a boat creaks…

◆ ◆ ◆ ◆ ◆

SCENE FIVE

ROSE: I'm eight and I'm just getting better. At five-thirty in the morning, Dad wakes me up to go crayfishing. I rub the sleep out of my eyes and climb into the car still in my pink pyjamas. We drive down to the marina, across the road from Kentucky Fried, near that big famous merry-go-round in the sea, and I help Dad unwinch the boat into the water.

The water is so cold it feels like ants nipping at my legs. Dad holds the boat still as I wade in up to my knees, holding my pyjamas high, and hoist myself into the boat. Then I put on my life jacket. It smells rotten and has chunky flecks of fish guts on it… Dad helps me buckle it, and I see the scar white and raised on his hand as he nooses the strap around and through the catch.

Dad doesn't wear a life jacket. He wouldn't be so stupid as to fall overboard and get his Winfields wet. He stands at the wheel and looks like a pirate biting down hard on his cigarette and squinting at the whipping wind. I hold onto my hair. It's just coming back and I don't want it to blow away. Dad revs the boat and it goes faster and faster and we fly past the buoys that bob up and down in the water.

We stop at the first pot. Bright orange with big sloppy numbers painted on it.

I like watching Dad pull the pots in. Like he's dancing with himself. The long, wet rope gets darker and murkier in colour and his arms begin to strain and tremble as he pulls it in from the deep blackness. I stand up on wobbly sea legs and try to help him. As the rope gets taut it feels like barbed wire cutting through my hands but I don't let go— [*moving a bar table to centre stage*] —not until the pot explodes out of the water and onto the floor of the boat, full of bright red bodies.

BRIAN*'s voice calls out…*

BRIAN: Scared of something, Dannyboy?
ROSE: The crayfish!

SCENE SIX

A lighting shift and ROSE *is back in the house.* DANNY *and* BRIAN *are still facing off.*

DANNY: I'm not fucking scared, Da. I just don't want to go.
BRIAN: Do you hear this, Rosey? Your Da's too important now. Can't find time for a pint in his old local with his poor ol' da.

DANNY: Da, I've just come from Australia to see you. We've got plenty of whiskey here. We don't need a pint at the Fox.

BRIAN: I always have a pint at the Fox, Danny. In memory of what happened there. Told them all you were coming, I did. They're expecting you.

ROSE: What did happen there?

DANNY: I don't want to go to the Fox. Boys will be round soon anyway.

BRIAN: Hasn't changed, you know, Danny. Same people sitting at the bar. Same old smells, same old stories. Stories about you, Dannyboy.

ROSE: What stories?

DANNY: Leave it, Rose. Da, enough.

BRIAN: Had his last drink in England at that pub, Rosey, before he paid his ten pounds and headed to Australian waters.

DANNY: Aye. My *last* drink in that bar.

BRIAN: His last drink with his brothers.

DANNY: My last drink because of my brothers.

> ROSE *gets out the dictaphone, puts it on the mantelpiece. She presses record.*

ROSE: Go on, Dad.

> *An awkward beat.* DANNY *takes a drink.*

BRIAN: There's still marks on the carpet, Danny. Right by the bar.

DANNY: Jesus, Da. They could be from anything.

BRIAN: And how would you know? You never went back there after that, Danny. I did. And those marks have been there since that very night.

> ROSE *looks to her father.*

ROSE: What are they? The marks.

BRIAN: Bloodstains, Rosey. Blood.

ROSE: Dad?

BRIAN: Bloodstains.

> ROSE *asks her father again…*

ROSE: What happened?

BRIAN: Out for a night with the boys, that's all. His brothers. My merry men. Out fishing.

DANNY: Leave it, Da.

BRIAN: They used to go to the Fox because Trevor liked a bird behind the bar. Linda. Blonde. Big green eyes. Tits from here to kingdom come—right, Dannyboy?

DANNY: I said leave it.

BRIAN: The Maloney boys. Baby Paddy, Mad Malachy, Trevor and his muscles, this one, and Colm. Me oldest. Red-headed like his mam. You'll meet him soon.

DANNY It's not important now.

He switches off the dictaphone.

ROSE: Dad…

BRIAN: Not important? You selfish little bastard. It was the night that changed everything for this family. For you, Danny.

He switches the dictaphone back on.

DANNY: I said it's not important anymore, Da! Just leave it!

He switches it off. BRIAN *switches it back on.* DANNY *grabs it again, takes the tape out and breaks it. Beat.* BRIAN *glares at* DANNY *who swigs his drink.* ROSE *gets her dictaphone and the broken tape.*

ROSE: Granddad, any shops around here?

BRIAN: There's a Tescos up the road, ducky.

ROSE: That'll do. Back soon.

She takes a long hard look at her dad. He ignores her stare. She leaves.

BRIAN: Not important? You fucking bastard. I lost my boys that night, Danny.

DANNY: You weren't there, Da. You don't know what happened.

BRIAN: I know there was a little scrap and one of my boys ran away. Left his brothers to get the blame. Tsk, tsk, tsk.

DANNY: It wasn't like that, Da.

BRIAN: The little runt ran away.

DANNY: You weren't there!

Beat. They both drink.

I remember thinking Colm must've hurt himself at work. When we left the house that night, he was walking funny. Sort of stiff. And he was in a foul mood. Scowling at anyone who passed us.

BRIAN: That's just his way, Danny.

DANNY: When we got here there was a table spare. There usually was— people tended to vacate seats when the Maloneys were out for the night.

BRIAN *smiles, pleased.*

But Colm didn't want to sit. Wanted to stand at the bar. Pint after pint after pint—Colm kept glaring at this bunch of blokes on the other side of the pub.

BRIAN: Those fucking Notts County supporters.

DANNY: Colm kept thudding his glass down, glaring at them. And then I don't know who moved first, but suddenly both Colm and a Prod were in the bar and Linda the barmaid was screaming. I looked up and saw that Colm had a pint glass coming out of his face. Literally. It was embedded around his mouth and chin. There was still some Guinness in it, mixing with the blood that was pissing out of his eyes and nose like he was finishing his pint, and bleeding snot into it at the same time.

BRIAN: I know what happened to him! He's still got the fucking scars.

DANNY: And then I saw the Protestant Notts County supporter had an axe sticking out of his back. Straight and deep between his shoulder blades, splitting his vertebrae in half, high, near his neck. He was screaming. And Colm's hand was still on the handle.

BRIAN *takes a long drink.*

The last thing I thought before the barstool knocked me out was how did Colm move so fast with that stiff leg? [*Beat.*] It was the axe, you see. He had that axe down his trouser leg. Planned the whole thing.

BRIAN: They were out for a night on the town, that's all. My merry men. And where did they end up? The Borstals. My little boys locked away by an English judge because they stood up for being Irish Catholic Nottingham Forest supporters. The only one who got off was you, Danny. You didn't fight the fight.

DANNY: I was unconscious under a table, Da! They left me there!

BRIAN: No! You left them! While they were getting locked away you got your ten pounds out of your little secret piggy bank and ran away to Australia. Deserter. Those marks are your family's blood, Danny. Your family's blood.

DANNY: My family? So where are they, then?

BRIAN: They're coming. They've got a bone to pick with their brother.

ROSE *enters and quietly tries to insert a tape into her dictaphone.*

DANNY: Fuck that. I've just travelled ten thousand miles to see them.

BRIAN: You watch your tongue, Dannyboy. Two visits in forty years doesn't make you a fucking martyr.

And the tape clicks in.

Switch that fucking thing off.

ROSE *switches it off and moves to them.*

ROSE: What were you talking about? What did I miss?

BRIAN: It's not important.

BRIAN *goes to the radio and switches it on loud. The races are on. He gives* ROSE *a betting slip and a racing guide.*

There you are, Rosey. Put a bet on for you.

ROSE: Thanks, Granddad.

BRIAN: Figured you need a bit of luck, ducky.

ROSE *stares at him. He smiles at her sweetly. She looks at her ticket.*

ROSE: Number seven. Which one is that?

BRIAN: Have a look.

ROSE *looks at the newspaper.*

ROSE: Rambling Rosey!

BRIAN: You know who owns that horse, Rosey? Your Uncle Malachy.

DANNY: What? Malachy owns a racehorse?

BRIAN: He's not as mad as he comes across, Danny. Invests all his earnings into the track. This one's his latest. Likes to name them after members of the family.

ROSE: But he's never even met me.

BRIAN: When you're a Maloney you're a Maloney. Besides, Rose is a nice name for a horse.

The race begins.

DANNY: But Malachy's a fucking madman! He can't even read.

BRIAN: Watch your tongue. That's your brother you're talking about. Don't need to be able to read to be able to count. Don't need to be able to read to drive an Audi.

DANNY: Malachy's got an Audi as well?

BRIAN: He'll be round later. Can take you for a spin.

DANNY: How many horses does he own?

BRIAN: Lots and lots. All named after his family. Trevor's Triumph, Majestic Maisie, Proud Paddy, Courage of Colm, Brian the Brave and Danny's Disgrace.

DANNY: What?

BRIAN: That last one got put down just recently. Lame.

Rambling Rosey has won.

ROSE: Granddad! I won!

BRIAN: At least someone here's a winner. You'll have to go and collect your winnings, Rosey. Bookie's on the corner.

ROSE: How much did you put on it, Granddad?

BRIAN: One hundred.

ROSE: So how much do I get back?

BRIAN: At three-to-one you get back… three pounds.

ROSE: Three pounds?

BRIAN: Aye. One hundred p at three-to-one gives you three pound return.

ROSE: Well, I guess that's almost ten bucks in Australia. Ta… Grandda.

BRIAN: A pleasure, Rosey. Plenty more where that came from with your surname in this town. That's just a taster. Your luck's changing, Rosey.

ROSE: I reckon it is.

DANNY *can't take any more.*

BRIAN: Bookie's on the corner, Rosey-posey.

DANNY: I'm going to get some fresh air.

He goes outside. ROSE *goes to leave, too, with her betting slip. Before she can exit…*

BRIAN: Rosey—do me a favour—give the man this when he gives you your money.

He stands with his hand in his pocket.

ROSE: What is it?

BRIAN: Just something owing to him.

ROSE: What sort of something?

BRIAN: Just give him this and you'll get more than three pounds in your palm.

She looks at him suspiciously.

Rosey… I'm your grandda and I'm a gambling man. I'm hardly going to blow up the bookie's, am I? Especially on the fifth of November.

ROSE *goes to him cautiously, links her arm with his and discreetly takes the package from his pocket.*

I'd do it myself, my darling, but sometimes I can't stand the excitement. My bladder turns eighty today too, remember. Just do your poor old incontinent grandda a favour and give a present to the nice bookie man. [*He smiles at* ROSE.] In any case it'll make a good story.

She looks at the package, then once more at BRIAN, *then leaves.*

SCENE SEVEN

Outside, DANNY *takes out a cigarette and gets out a smoke. We hear a distant starter gun/penny bunger going off. There is a red glow. A low rumbling.* DANNY *starts to tremble violently. The cigarette drops to the ground and he goes very still—in a kind of trance.*

Inside, BRIAN *hears the explosions and laughs gleefully. He takes off his jacket.*

BRIAN: Remember, remember the fifth of November.
          The gunpowder, treason and plot.
          I see of no reason why gunpowder treason
          Should ever be forgot.
          Guy Fawkes, Guy Fawkes, 'twas his intent
          To blow up the King and the Parliament,
          Three score barrels of powder below
          To prove old England's overthrow,
          By dark providence he was catch'd
          With a dark lantern and burning match.
          Hip hoorah…
          Hip-hip hoorah
          Hip-hip hip-hip hoorah…

Outside, DANNY *is having a whiteout.*

DANNY: Rose!

          Inside, ROSE *runs into the house. She is breathless.* DANNY *remains outside, mid-whiteout.*

ROSE: What was in that package? He just gave me two hundred pounds for it!

BRIAN: Did it feel good? Did you get a rush, Rose?

Outside...

DANNY: Rose!

Inside...

BRIAN: Did you get a little skip in your heart? Goosebumps on your flesh, Rosey?

Outside...

DANNY: Rosey!

Inside...

BRIAN: I knew you were one of us, Rosey. Tingles, hey? One of us!

ROSE: What did I just do?

BRIAN: You just cashed in my pools winnings from the past year. Not a bad twelve months really.

ROSE: Pools winnings?

BRIAN: Aye, Rose. The lottery.

ROSE: I thought that was a... I thought I was giving that man...

> *Beat.* DANNY *comes to. He leans down and picks up his cigarette, then exits.*

BRIAN: Rat poison...? Animal tranquilisers?

> *She is exhilarated.*

No, Rosey. That's next week.

> *He embraces her tightly.*

You did the job like a real soldier of the streets. Good girl. You did your family proud. Like a true Maloney.

> ROSE *beams, embracing him tightly too.* DANNY *re-enters. He sees them embracing.*

DANNY: Ey-up!

BRIAN & ROSE: [*together*] Ey-up!

DANNY: Get much back?

ROSE: Enough for a couple more tapes, at least.

> *An explosion. Loud and close.* DANNY *reacts violently.*

What is that?

> *Another explosion.*

BRIAN: The celebrations have begun, Rosey.

DANNY: [*to himself*] Bonfire night.

BRIAN: It's starting to get dark now so the bonfires and fireworks and parades are starting for our Guy.

ROSE: Fantastic! Let's go and watch!

BRIAN: The Maloneys don't partake in the celebration of a brother's demise, Rosey. We don't burn Guy Fawkes at the stake. We don't parade him through town and laugh at his misfortune and then set fire to his straw balls like the English do.

More fireworks. DANNY *winces.*

DANNY: They're just fireworks.

BRIAN: We'll stay here and celebrate Guy Fawkes Night the Maloney way. With your uncles.

More explosions. DANNY *looks terrified.*

ROSE: Are you okay, Dad?

BRIAN: What's wrong with you, Danny?

DANNY: I'm fine, Da. The boys will be round soon, Rose.

BRIAN: Look at him—it's freezing out there and he's sweating a river!

DANNY: They're on their way.

BRIAN: Are you ready, Rose? Time to meet the rest of your family.

SCENE EIGHT

A lighting and sound shift. We are back on the boat again with ROSE.

ROSE: Dad measures the crayfish with an Emu Export can. If the cray's torso comes over the emu's beak, it's a good size and is coming home with us. Any less than the beak, then it's a cacker and I get to throw it back. I like searching for the cackers in the mounds of red bodies. I like to spot the weak ones and send them back to the sea—to their home.

I put my hand in the pot and fish them out carefully by their long, thorny antennae and try to keep my fingers away from their backsides. I've seen the scars on fisherman's hands from the poisonous cuts left by crays. I don't want any more scars on me.

I try to throw the cackers back as gently as possible. But they always look shocked when they hit the water—still for a moment on the surface before they thrust themselves away.

An orange smudge in the murky green. And then onto the next pot we go.

She finds a box of photos and letters beneath her grandda's chair. She rifles through them as she speaks.

You never know what you're going to get when the pot bursts through the water. Some days it might be full of crays, clacking angrily and screaming. Sometimes an octopus that pisses ink all over our ankles. Even when Dad chops their head off they have perfect aim and can hit you in the eye with one purple squirt. The deck beneath our feet speckled with black spots as it wriggles, headless, across the boat. Or sometimes we'll get a baby shark glaring at us through the rungs of the pot.

DANNY *enters and pours himself a long drink.* ROSE *sees him.*

You just never know what you're gonna get out there.

DANNY *drinks.* ROSE *watches him.*

And sometimes you need more than a life jacket to get you through it.

◆ ◆ ◆ ◆ ◆

SCENE NINE

Still inside Brian's flat. DANNY *is sitting in Brian's chair, drinking.* BRIAN *enters and stops at the sight of* DANNY *seated.*

BRIAN: That's my fucking chair, Dannyboy.

DANNY *gets up from the chair.*

Bit of respect wouldn't go astray, boy.

BRIAN *leaves.* DANNY *sees* ROSE *is rifling through a glory box. He drinks.* BRIAN *re-enters and puts a straw Guy Fawkes in the chair. He gives him a Guinness.*

Rosey, say hello to your Uncle Guy.

ROSE: Hello, Uncle Guy.

DANNY: At least someone in this family hasn't got any older.

Fireworks continue to whiz and bang throughout scene. ROSE *rifles through the small box of old letters.*

ROSE: 'Dear Mam, Da, Colm, Trevor, Malachy and Paddy.'
DANNY: What's that?
ROSE: It's your handwriting, Dad. Found it.
BRIAN: Pokey-nose.
DANNY: You shouldn't touch, Rose.

ROSE *goes back to the letters.*

ROSE: 'I have arrived in Geraldton…'
BRIAN: Your ma kept your letters. Bloody woman never could throw anything away.

Fireworks.

DANNY: Leave it, Rose!
ROSE: 'It is on the west coast of Australia, a long way from anywhere. It's very hot here but very windy. The trees all bend over and touch the ground like they're bowing to meet you. Or praying.' Dad, you sound so young!
DANNY: I was young. Nineteen. Put them away now, Rose.
BRIAN: When I was nineteen I was doing more important things than looking at bent trees…

She reads again.

ROSE: 'I'm working hard on the roads. I have a "ute"—a type of Australian car—and every morning I wake up early and drive to all sorts of funny-sounding places—Yalgoo, Mullewa, Marble Bar, Dongara. It's very hard work. You wouldn't recognise me—I'm dark brown—'
BRIAN: Turned into an aboriginality.
ROSE: 'And I've got a moustache—just like you, Da.'
BRIAN: Had mine from age fourteen, Rosey.
DANNY: Got rid of mine.
BRIAN: Fell out, more like.
ROSE: 'I've met some nice people in Geraldton. They take me crayfishing on weekends. Crayfish are a kind of lobster and are delicious in sandwiches.'
BRIAN: Showing off with his catfish sandwiches knowing full well how hungry his brothers must be in the Borstals…

Fireworks.

ROSE: 'But I am very homesick. I don't understand this country. They're at war but I can't work out what for and I'm too embarrassed to ask.

It's somewhere in South-East Asia. Is it on the news over there? I've been called up to—'

DANNY *strides over to take the letters but* ROSE *snatches them from his reach.*

DANNY: Enough, Rose.

ROSE: They're not yours, Dad.

DANNY: They're more mine than yours.

ROSE: Grandda, can I please read them?

They both look to BRIAN.

BRIAN: They're not important.

She gives in. DANNY *takes the letters and puts them in his pocket. Beat. Fireworks.* ROSE *goes back to the box. She pulls out a photo.*

ROSE: Look! It's me when I was sick.

DANNY *looks at the photo.*

DANNY: [*smiling*] My little Baldilocks.

ROSE: Look at Mum. She'd be my age there.

DANNY: She was. Too young to go through that.

BRIAN: Show me that photo, Rosey.

She does.

My little poorly granddaughter. Was St Bernadette that got you better, Rosey. We prayed to her every night.

DANNY: I think it was two years in hospital that got her better, Da.

BRIAN: What was the hospital's name? Princess Margaret? Imagine naming a hospital after that fucking tart.

DANNY: What do you suggest, Da? The Sinn Fein Hospital for Children?

BRIAN: Don't be stupid, Danny. St Bernadette is a much better name. Patron saint of the poorly.

DANNY: Patron saint of embarrassing middle names, more like.

BRIAN *whacks him.*

BRIAN: You be proud of your name, you little prat. Your da's embarrassed of his middle name.

ROSE: Dad doesn't have a middle name.

BRIAN: Like fuck he doesn't. He's Danny Bernadette Maloney. I'm Brian Bernadette Maloney.

ROSE *bursts out laughing.*

So you're Rose Bernadette Maloney.

ROSE: My middle name's Maree. I don't have a confirmation name.

BRIAN: Your confirmation name's the most important name of all, Rosey Bernadette. You be proud of it.

ROSE: Granddad, that's not my name. I'm not Catholic.

Fireworks.

BRIAN: What did you say? What did she say?

DANNY: She said she's not Catholic.

Beat. More fireworks. BRIAN *looks at her stunned.* DANNY *takes a long swig of his beer.* BRIAN *pulls out a scrapbook of photos.*

BRIAN: Look at this photo here, Rosey. You see?

ROSE *looks closely at the photo.*

See that babby being held by the priest? That's you. Me and your mammar got that photo in the post. Our little Australian granddaughter. Baptised. Rose Maree Maloney.

ROSE *looks confused.*

Look a little further along now. Ten years on. There you are. Little stain by your mouth there. You've just drunk the blood of Christ. Eaten his flesh.

ROSE *looks at her father.*

And now look a little further on. Your Confirmation. You've accepted the mystery of the Holy Ghost. You're now Rose Maree Bernadette Maloney till the day you die. So don't you tell me you're not a Catholic. You've climbed every rung so far and I've got the holy Kodaks to prove it.

ROSE *continues to look at the photos, confused.*

DANNY: How can you 'accept a mystery'? It's like saying, 'I accept the bunyip'.

BRIAN: What the fuck is a bunyip?

DANNY: Forget about it, Da.

Fireworks. ROSE *is still taking in the scrapbook.*

ROSE: I remember this photo. I thought I looked like a bride. But I don't remember anything about eating the flesh of God. Ugh… disgusting.

BRIAN: Jesus, Mary and Joseph. I hope He's taking a bath so He doesn't hear this blasphemer daughter of yours, Danny.

DANNY: Of course he's taking a bath, Da. He's in a big bath on a lovely fluffy cloud with Mary Poppins and they're all playing harps and sacrificing lambs and turning blood into bread and having a big orgasmic Catholic experience.

BRIAN: You'll be damned, man. You should be ashamed speaking that way. Cover his ears, Rosey.

ROSE: What?

BRIAN: [*pointing at Guy Fawkes*] Cover his ears!

ROSE: He doesn't have any.

BRIAN: Lucky bastard. Cover his eyes, then.

ROSE: Why?

BRIAN: So he doesn't have to witness what I'm about to do to both you blasphemers.

> *Fireworks.*

DANNY: Oh, come on, Da. You're not Catholic.

BRIAN: Like fuck I'm not Catholic. That's our fucking fight. That's *your* fucking fight, Rose.

DANNY: Bullshit, Da. Rose isn't Catholic.

BRIAN: [*the photos*] Well, what are all these about, then?

DANNY: They're all set-ups. That's not even a real priest. It was the goal-keeper from my soccer team.

BRIAN: You ought to be ashamed, Danny Maloney. Using the Holy Spirit to pose for a photograph. Using your daughter to kiss the arse of your father. Wipe your mouth, Rosey, you're not a real Catholic.

> ROSE *sits back down. The fireworks rise in intensity.*

DANNY: And you are, Da?

BRIAN: We all are in this family.

DANNY: When was the last time you went to Mass, Da?

BRIAN: I go to different sermons than most.

DANNY: Sermons down back alleys where you drink the blessed Guinness and read from the book of McKevitt?

BRIAN: Book of McKevitt?

DANNY: Mickey McKevitt, Da. With his wife Bernadette.

BRIAN: I know who they are! I've devoted my life to the Irish, my boy. You've done fuck-all for our cause. Don't you stand in judgement.

DANNY: Your cause? Let me ask you about your cause, Da. What's the difference between a Roman Catholic and an Irish Catholic? I'll tell you the difference—one fucks children in the name of God and one kills children in the name of God.

    BRIAN *and* ROSE *are shocked.*

Now, you see, our family was baptised Irish Catholic in Roman Catholic churches, so what does that make us? Should we fuck them then kill them or kill them then fuck them?

ROSE: Dad, you're drunk. That's enough.

BRIAN: There's no hope for you, Rosey. Not with this fucker as a father.

    Fireworks. DANNY *snaps.*

DANNY: Don't you damn my daughter!

BRIAN: She's already damned. Fucking priest should have drowned you when he had the chance.

DANNY & ROSE: [*together*] Who? Me or him/her?

BRIAN: Either or.

    A long beat. Then... there is a loud knock at the door. They all stare at each other, stunned. BRIAN *smiles sweetly.*

Ey-up. It's your brothers.

    Blackout.

END OF ACT ONE

ACT TWO

SCENE ONE

BRIAN *and* DANNY *stand in the same positions they were left in at the end of Act One. After a beat,* ROSE *enters, carrying a bunch of flowers. They all look at them confused. The card says nothing.*

BRIAN: They must be from the boys.
DANNY: Interflora?
ROSE: They must be from Mum.

> *She dials her phone.*

BRIAN: No, no. They're from the boys. Some sort of signal.

> *He grabs the flowers and tears them apart, searching.*

DANNY: Must've cost a fortune.
ROSE: What time is it in Geraldton?
BRIAN: I'll bet they've hidden something in here. A package. Or something.
ROSE: [*on the phone*] Hello, Mum? Can you hear me?
BRIAN: Have to disguise things, you see. Keep pokey-noses out.
DANNY: Careful, Da…
ROSE: [*on the phone*] We're fine. Did you send us flowers? [*To* DANNY *and* BRIAN] They're from Mum. [*On the phone*] Yeah—they got here just now.

> BRIAN *has demolished the flowers.* ROSE *looks at them.*

They're beautiful, Mum. Really beautiful… He's fine. I'll put him on.

> ROSE *passes the phone to* DANNY *but* BRIAN *intercepts it, shoving the flowers at* ROSE.

BRIAN: [*on the phone*] Ey-up, Glenys! It's Brian here…! Yes—got them, thank you… Yes, good to see them both—about fucking time—thought you had them under lock and key. Like true Australian convicts… Why'd you not come, ducky, the Maloney's not good enough for you? Too Catholic maybe…? Well, you took

our name as well as our Danny, least you could do is come and visit
once a century... No, no—not here yet. On their way... He's here,
yes. [*Beat.*] Oh, you want to talk to him? Fair enough. [*To* DANNY]
Danny, it's your wife... [*Back on the phone*] Cheerio, Glenys. All
my love to the sharks down there.

DANNY *gets on.*

DANNY: [*on the phone*] G'day, duck...! Good. Everything's good.
We're just waiting for the boys. Thought your flowers were them...
Just gone six but it's already dark. Guy Fawkes parade just passed...
Yeah, there were a few. But I'm all right... [*He looks at his father.*]
He's all right too... Yeah. Yeah. Just talking. Catching up on old
times... Everything's all right. I'm all right. She's all right... Her
and her grandda are getting on like nothing else... I'll put her back
on. You can talk to her yourself... Ta, duck. You too.

ROSE *gets back on the phone.*

ROSE: [*on the phone*] Hi... Yes. I'm fine. I'm great... Has Charles
called...?

Her father and grandfather see her disappointed face.

Just asking...

She leaves the room. BRIAN *peers after her.*

BRIAN: Bloody women. Never let you listen in.
DANNY: I'm sorry, Da. About before.
BRIAN: What's she doing in there?
DANNY: I fly off the handle sometimes...
BRIAN: Can't hear a word she's saying...
DANNY: Just like you, Da.
BRIAN: Quiet, Dannyboy, I want to listen.

DANNY *rolls his eyes.*

DANNY: She keeps herself to herself, Da. Prefers other people's stories.
BRIAN: She's too thin, you know.
DANNY: She's had a tough year.
BRIAN: She should be out having fun. Getting up to mischief.
DANNY: She's not in the mood for any of that, Da.
BRIAN: What did he do to her, this Charles?
DANNY: Nothing, Da.

BRIAN: Like fuck. They were getting married a month ago. I'll ask her myself, shall I?

DANNY: He left her, Da. Leave her alone.

BRIAN: Left her? What did she do?

DANNY: Nothing.

BRIAN: Bullshit. Pretty girl like her. Always a spare card up the sleeve.

DANNY: No, Da.

BRIAN: Him, then? Andrew. Did he fuck around on my granddaughter? Fuckin prat!

DANNY: No, Da.

BRIAN: Bloody useless, you are… I'll ask her myself.

He stands…

DANNY: Da! Don't.

BRIAN *glares at him.* DANNY *sighs.*

Please. Leave her alone.

BRIAN: My granddaughter, she is. She came all this way to see me and you won't even let us get to know each other.

DANNY: You're getting to know each other just fine without bringing all that up.

BRIAN: She's all right, isn't she? Not poorly again? It hasn't come back, has it?

DANNY: No, Da.

BRIAN: I tried to save my pennies to visit when she was poorly. You know that, don't you, Dannyboy?

DANNY: Was twenty-five years ago, Da. Forget about it.

BRIAN: Tried to save my pennies. But you were all so fucking far away. Broke my heart it did, Danny. Photos of Rose with no hair and that big scar across her belly and so small in that hospital bed. My only grandchild. Dying.

DANNY: Try to forget, Da.

BRIAN: Never heard of such a thing. A three-year-old with kidney cancer.

DANNY: She wasn't three, Da. She was born with it. We just didn't find out for a few years.

BRIAN: Broke my heart, it did. Broke my fucking heart.

DANNY *is silent.*

'Course you never did have any luck with the little ones. How many
did you lose before Rose?

DANNY: Four, Da. Four miscarriages.

BRIAN: Something wrong with her insides. Glenys.

DANNY: Wasn't Glenys' fault, Da.

BRIAN: Bled out of her body, didn't they?

DANNY: It didn't come from Glenys, Da. I brought something inside
me back from Vietnam. Something I breathed in. Agent Orange.

BRIAN: Agent Orange? The fuck is that?

DANNY: A spray, Da. A defoliant. We used to spray it over the trees so
the enemies had nowhere to hide. Rained down on all of us, it did.
And we breathed it in and brought it back with us.

BRIAN: Is that right, Dannyboy?

DANNY: It's right, Da. We all know it. All my mates are dropping off from
leukaemia. The rest of us are covered in rashes. Suffering migraines,
blackouts. Whiteouts. Our wives have their insides ruined. Our
children are born with harelips and their feet back-to-front and their
spines half grown and tumours in their bellies. And that's if they're
lucky.

BRIAN: What are they doing for you, Danny? Are they helping you down
there?

DANNY: They have a proud history of denial in Australia, Da. The
government back then were in on it, you see. The Agent Orange.
And the same ones that sent us there, the same ones that tested the
stuff for the Yanks, are the same ones that deny there's any problem
at all. They've never told us the full story.

BRIAN: Then fucking make them.

DANNY: They're too busy doing it all again, Da. Easier to sweep us all
under the carpet, generation by generation.

BRIAN: Orange spray? Jesus, Mary and Joseph. I thought the English had
a stupid government but your lot down there, Danny, they take the
fucking cake. That's what fighting for the Crown gets you, Danny.
Idiots. Who ever heard of fighting a war with a garden hose?

DANNY: Could be worse. Could throw potatoes at each other.

BRIAN: Watch your mouth, son.

DANNY: Chemicals are chemicals, Da. The damage they do is more than
any bullets or bayonets.

BRIAN: Still, a good soldier fights with what he's given. Be it substance or steel, his hands or his heart.

DANNY: Do you believe that, Da?

BRIAN: I do, Dannyboy.

DANNY: But when does the fight end?

BRIAN: When the war is won.

DANNY: What about when the war is lost?

BRIAN: You never lose a war, Danny. It follows you home. Stuck to your soul.

DANNY: Is yours stuck to your soul, Da?

BRIAN: We didn't lose.

DANNY: You never exactly won it either.

BRIAN: Because the fight's not over yet. I'm still a soldier. I'll never give up my cause. My pride. [*He smiles at* DANNY.] But you're a different soldier to me, Danny, aren't you? That's what fighting for the Crown will do to you. Poisons your soul and your seed. [*Beat.*] I've watched you, Danny. I've noticed. You're not like me. You're

Martin Vaughan (left) as Brian and Danny Adcock as Danny in the 2007 Mimmam production in Sydney. (Photo: Brett Boardman)

a little bit too nervous. A little bit funny, aren't you? I've noticed you sitting over there, drinking and drinking and drinking, jumping at loud noises, shaking, sweating. I see the lines on your face, Dannyboy. I see your red eyes and your haggard cheeks and your dull soul and the imprints on your conscience. You look a million years old, my guilty son, because you know you chose the wrong crusade. You chose to fight for the Crown instead of against it. You're a different soldier to me and Robin Hood and Guy Fawkes. We can sleep well in our beds at night. You're full of poison while we're full of pride. We're all courage and you're all...

DANNY: [*softly*] ... chemicals.

BRIAN: I know fucking chemicals. Did you come across Semtex in Vienna, Soldier Danny?

DANNY: Vietnam, Da.

BRIAN: That's what I said.

DANNY: I didn't know what I was touching half the time.

BRIAN: I've always used Semtex, Danny. Almost got caught smuggling it into a meeting in The Meadows as a young lad. All the boys were in there waiting for me to deliver it. It's dangerous stuff, Danny. Very volatile. The pigs pulled me up, threw me against a wall and searched me. All over. Up me shirt. Down me pants. Up me arsehole. Fortunately I'd had the good sense to put it in a sugar bag amongst some groceries so they found nowt. Let me go on my way. Stupid bastards.

DANNY: Why'd they search you if you were just walking along with your groceries?

BRIAN: 'Cause I'm Irish. And a Maloney.

DANNY: So what happened to the Semtex?

BRIAN: I got it to the boys and it was used in the very next bombing.

DANNY: Where was that?

BRIAN: One of many.

DANNY: And you always used Semtex, Da?

BRIAN: My explosive of choice. After gunpowder, of course.

DANNY: How many have you killed, Da?

BRIAN: More than you can count, boy.

DANNY: More than eighty.

BRIAN: More than I care to talk about. Maybe if you'd fought on my side I'd share. Maybe if you weren't scared of loud noises.

DANNY: I'm not scared of loud noises.

BRIAN: Oh, just fireworks, is it? All the scary purple and orange colours. Poor Dannyboy. Poor, poor babby.

DANNY: I'm not scared of loud noises.

BRIAN: Of course you're not. *Bang!*

> DANNY *leaps.* BRIAN *laughs.*

Bang!

DANNY: Shut up, Da!

BRIAN: [*whispering*] Bang.

> *He smiles sweetly at* DANNY. ROSE *enters.*

ROSE: What's going on? What did I miss?

DANNY: I'm just going to call your mother again. Forgot to tell her something.

> *He goes.* BRIAN *giggles to himself.*

♦ ♦ ♦ ♦ ♦

SCENE TWO

BRIAN: Moody bastard.

> ROSE *calls after her father.*

ROSE: Dad?

BRIAN: I've got a story for you, Rosey. One for your book. One of my own.

ROSE: Dad!

BRIAN: What, you're too important to listen to your poor old grandda's story? My life not interesting enough, Rosey?

ROSE: No, Granddad. Grandda.

BRIAN: He'll never tell, Rosey. Never even confided in his dear old mam about what happened over there. He's got nothing to say. [*He appeals to her.*] But I do, ducky.

> *She is hesitant.*

I used to watch your mammar write those letters to your da. I loved the way she scratched away at the page. All flushed with gossipy thoughts and best wishes and yearning for her Dannyboy. You remind me so much of her, Rosey.

She smiles.

Let me tell you a story, my granddaughter. We can have fun, you and I. I'll give you what you want.

ROSE *looks for her father again.*

He's all right.

She smiles at her grandfather. He invites her to sit. She does.

My mate Joe and I were the principal bomb-makers for this part of this godforsaken country. I was chosen for my cast-iron courage for the cause, whilst Joe was chosen for his long, nimble fingers. I'd sketch the bombs and gather the required parts and Joe would put it together. We'd meet every Sunday after Mass, me and Joe, at a top-secret location down by Sherwood Castle. It was there that we'd make the bombs. I'd bring all the ingredients and Joe with his nimble little fingers would fix it all into a nice little package for our English enemies.

Now, Rosey, the making of a bomb, from original sketch to the planting of it in a public arena could take months, even years. So to pass the time, I came up with a little hobby every time Joe and I would sit down to work. First of all, I'd set out all the nails and wires and Semtex into nice, neat piles for Joe. Then I'd quietly stand behind him holding the plans and instruct him as to what went where and how. I'd then wait until he was knuckle-deep in barbed wires and nails and chemicals. *Bang!* I'd yell.

ROSE *leaps on the 'Bang!'* BRIAN *laughs.*

That's exactly what he did! Leapt like a little girl skipping rope! *Bang!* I'd yell it over and over—right when he least expected it! *Bang! Bang!*

He laughs. ROSE *doesn't know what to think.*

And every time I'd convince him that I wouldn't do it again, it wasn't funny, and that we should just get on with the job. And then every time he'd go back in with those long, nimble fingers I'd yell it. *Bang! Bang! Bang! Bang!* Till he was shaking and sweating and crying for me to stop.

They both laugh. ROSE, *a little reluctantly, but encouraged by her grandfather's delight.*

So one day, we was all ready to go. Joe put the bomb in a bag and we were going to leave it on a train bound for London. Same line that you just came in on. [*Beat.*] But he did the strangest thing, Rosey. As we walked to the train station, me a fair way ahead so as not to be associated with one another, he called out my name. He called out my fucking name, Rosey, for all in the street to hear. I turned round. And there stood Joe in the middle of the street, holding the bomb in his fucking hands. In full view. In those long nimble fingers. 'Bang!' he whispered. And detonated the fucker.

     ROSE *is suddenly serious.*

ROSE: What?

BRIAN: *Bang!* He said.

ROSE: Granddad…

BRIAN: Grandda. *Bang!*

     Beat. ROSE *is stunned.*

What do you think, Rosey? A good story. You can have that one, my granddaughter.

     Beat.

ROSE: Grandda, that's… that's perfect. Can I tape that?

     BRIAN *nods. She runs to her bag to get her dictaphone.*

I can use it. I can use that. [*She rummages madly and then turns around.*] Right. Tell me again.

     She presses record. But her grandfather is asleep.

Grandda.

     He sleeps soundly. She spies the boxes and moves to them. She doesn't realise it, but her grandfather is watching her, although still lightly snoring. She starts quietly picking off the tape that is keeping the boxes closed. As she is about to open one up…

BRIAN: Fucking thief.

     ROSE *is startled.*

Thought you said you didn't like drugs.

ROSE: I don't. I'm not. I was just curious… I'll tape it back up.

     BRIAN *laughs.*

BRIAN: Catholic guilt. Gets you every time.

ROSE: Touché.

BRIAN: You like to take things, Rosey?

ROSE: No.

BRIAN: I can read you like a book, Rose. Thief.

ROSE: I'm not a thief.

BRIAN: And what about the things in your pocket?

ROSE: What things?

BRIAN: Inside your pockets you've got an ashtray from outside, two pens from the kitchen drawer, three letters of your mammar's, two family photographs, and some tapes from Tescos. On the table, please.

ROSE: That's ridiculous.

BRIAN: On the table, feather fingers.

> *Beat.* ROSE *gets out the items from various places in her clothing and places them on the table.*

ROSE: Don't tell Dad.

BRIAN: And the rest of it.

ROSE: That's it.

BRIAN: Rosey. Are you telling your dear old grandda you don't have twenty pounds of his winnings from the bookie's in your pocket?

> *A long beat.*

ROSE: It's not in my pocket.

> ROSE *gets the twenty-pound note from inside her bra and hands it to him.*

BRIAN: Hold onto it, Rosey. Buy yourself something nice.

> *She takes it back.*

And don't touch the boxes again, Rose. If it's drugs you're wanting, take these. They'll make you smile. Happy birthday from Grandda.

> *He holds out a packet from under his cushion.*

ROSE: I don't take drugs.

BRIAN: They'll help you sleep on the plane.

> *She takes them, pockets them.*

Where are you stopping on the way back?

ROSE: Singapore.

> BRIAN *snatches the pills back off her and puts them on his side table.*

BRIAN: Not every Maloney should end up in prison. Thief or not.

ROSE: [*smiling*] Grandda…

BRIAN: Yes, Rosey duck?

ROSE: How long has it been since Mammar died now?

BRIAN: Ten years.

ROSE: Do you miss her?

BRIAN: Like my soul.

ROSE: What do you miss most?

BRIAN: The little things I hated. Her smell. Her loudness. Her cheek. They're the things I miss most.

ROSE: Are you lonely here?

BRIAN: No.

ROSE: It's just that it's your birthday and nobody's turned up.

BRIAN: You have. And they're on their way. They can't wait to meet you. [*Beat.*] You miss your man?

ROSE *says nothing.*

That special, was he?

ROSE: Five years we were together.

BRIAN: Don't waste too much time mourning the bastard. You weren't given hips and tits for nowt, ducky. Get out there and use them to find yourself a good Catholic husband and then use them again for a babby. Don't you waste those Maloney genes, now. You're the only one left to carry on the name. Look at you. You're a fucking filly, Rambling Rosey, just like your mammar. Oh, what a mother she was. She loved her children more than life itself. Sang them to sleep, walked them to school, sat up the front at every Communion, every wedding, every court case. Maloney's are born mothers. It's criminal the way they love their children. So don't you let us down, Rosey. Look at you—all tits and arse and pretty smile. It's your turn to hold the flame now.

ROSE: Grandda. I can't have children.

BRIAN: What, girl?

ROSE: There was a spray that Dad breathed in and now I don't have the eggs. They've all been destroyed by radiotherapy and even if they found one, I can't carry it. The tumour wiped out half my organs, my body can't support a baby. Grandda, I'm thirty and I've just started menopause.

BRIAN: Well, now, that's where you need some faith, Rosey.

ROSE: I will never have children. [*Beat*.] I will never have children. [*Beat*.] I will never have children. And you know what? I don't think I deserve them anyway. When a friend tells me she's pregnant I smile and hug and kiss and ask her dumb questions. 'How far along?' 'Any names picked yet?' 'What are you craving?' But I don't let on what I'm craving. That despite my big smile and congratulations I'm green and I'm bubbling and I'm thinking, you bitch, I hope it fucking dies inside you, you bitch. And when a pregnant woman walks past me on the street I want to punch her belly and walk away when she falls to the ground and just leave her there to deal with it. And when a husband tells me he's having his third boy I want to put my hand down his pants and rip his fucking cock off and squeeze it dry of any seed. And when I see a baby in a pram... [*Beat*.] I just want to pick it up and smell its skin and hold it to my heart and stroke its little head and never let another person touch it for the rest of its life. Is that normal, Grandda? I don't know. And I never will. Because the seed stops here.

Beat.

BRIAN: I didn't know that, Rosey. About you and babbies. Nobody told me. Your da passed that onto you.

ROSE: It wasn't Dad. It was just the air he breathed in. [*Beat*.] But Charles knew from our first date that I couldn't have kids. It was never an issue until we were actually engaged.

BRIAN: And so he fucked off.

ROSE: And so he fucked off.

Beat.

BRIAN: And now you're making up stories, taking stories, taking ashtrays, taking anything to fill the hole in your belly.

ROSE *looks shocked.*

My only grandchild can't carry on my name. A fine name.

He holds out his arms. She goes to him. He holds her close.

My poor Rosey-posey. So like your mammar. So unlike your mammar.

He strokes her belly gently.

Poor little barren belly. Poor little poison seed. [*Beat.*] You stay here, Rosey. You stay here. You listen to your grandda, Rosey. We can make up for all that. You stay here. You've been put on this earth for another reason. I'll tell you your father's story, Rose. He's a turncoat, a deserter and a traitor. He's got no story worth telling. He's ashamed.

ROSE: It wasn't his fault. He was conscripted. He had no choice.

BRIAN: He had a choice, Rose. There's always choice. [*Beat.*] You have a choice now, too, Rosey. What are you going home with? An empty dickyphone and a pocketful of stolen blank tapes. Who are you going home to? A shit job and an empty house. And what's your other choice? The one God himself has given you.

ROSE: I don't believe in—

BRIAN: God's leading you towards a more important cause, Rosey, just like Mary all those years ago. Just like your mammar Maisie. He wants you to be the mother of the Maloneys. He knows we'll give you your stories. We'll fill up your belly with the answers you've always wanted. Because this is where your story really is, Rose. Here. Why start your story with him when you can start it with me? That's the choice you have right now.

♦ ♦ ♦ ♦ ♦

SCENE THREE

Lighting change. ROSE *turns to the audience.*

ROSE: Out this far, the water is colder and greener and saltier and crystal, crystal clear, like a big wet mirror. After I've thrown back the cackers, Dad holds out both his hands. 'Pick one,' he says. I choose the hand without the scar. Inside it is a red bow. Then Dad gets out a sack. Inside that is a dead dog. It's Bella from next door. Mrs Bagnato's terrier. Combed and shiny. Dad gets me to tie the bow around her neck. 'We're going to give it a sea burial,' he says, and throws the dog overboard with a small splash. 'Is Bella Catholic?' I say. Dad shrugs, exhales the last of his cigarette, and flicks it over the side of the boat. 'Ashes to ashes,' he says, then gives me my breakfast. A Mars Bar. 'Don't tell your mum.' I chomp down on it as we move onto the next pot, close my eyes, stroke the water's surface… and I catch a red ribbon. I look down and it's Bella, still bobbing in the water. Somehow she's followed us to the next pot. Her tongue is yellow and swollen and lapping dead in the water. I hold out the ribbon to Dad and out of nowhere he grabs an oar and pounds Bella over and over and over. But Bella won't sink. Then Dad leans over the edge of the boat and begins to tear Bella apart, ripping holes in, her to make her sink. I cry out, but it's like he can't hear me, won't hear me, until he's finished the job. And so he keeps pounding, pounding, pounding until Bella is swallowed by water. Waves of nausea weaken me. I throw up my Mars Bar and my father turns on me, and just for a moment, he's not my dad.

DANNY *enters and he and* ROSE *look at each other.*
He sits down and looks at me—through me—with those English, Irish, Australian eyes—and we bob up and down for a long time, in the middle of a massive black ocean.

SCENE FOUR

DANNY: Your mum says the paper called again. Something about getting their laptop off you?
BRIAN: Oooh!
DANNY: Rose—what laptop?
ROSE: My laptop? It's mine.

BRIAN *chuckles.*

DANNY: Well, they don't seem to think so. They said it belongs to the paper.
ROSE: It's mine.
BRIAN: A true Maloney, you are Rosey-posey. Hang onto it, I say.
DANNY: Don't start this trouble again, Rose.
ROSE: It's mine.

A long moment as they face off. She crumbles.

It's the least they could give me. Seven years of writing stories about kittens stuck in drains and junior soccer matches… You know one bloke who started at the same time as me is now a correspondent in Afghanistan. Afghanistan! And I'm still covering under-fourteens semi-finals.

DANNY: They also said you never resigned. You just stopped turning up for work.

ROSE *is silent.*

They had to get other people to cover for you.

ROSE: Dad, the work experience kid could cover for me.

DANNY: They were worried. Thought something had happened. Thought you might have…

ROSE: Might have.

Beat.

DANNY: They thought something had happened, that's all.

ROSE: Well, something did happen. I want to write for you, Dad. Not them.

DANNY: Don't use me as an excuse, Rose. You're here 'cause you ran away.

BRIAN: Like father, like daughter.

ROSE: I wasn't the one who ran away.

BRIAN: Was you who ran away, Dannyboy.

ROSE: Charles ran away.

BRIAN: Was you.

DANNY: Give the laptop back.

ROSE: Fine. I'm doing quite all right with a dickyphone anyway, aren't I, Grandda?

BRIAN *smiles.*

BRIAN: I'm going for a piss. Don't touch anything.

ROSE *and* DANNY *are left alone. An awkward silence.*

DANNY: You give that laptop back. It's not yours, Rose.

ROSE: I need it to write.

DANNY: What, like you needed that perfume from David Jones? Or the packet of sausages that you shoved down your pants at Woolworths? The nappy wipes? The baby food?

ROSE: The laptop is mine.

DANNY: Did you steal those tapes too, Rose?

Beat.

ROSE: You don't think I'm any good, do you, Dad?

DANNY: Rose, I don't understand why you feel you have to take things—

ROSE: I'm not talking about that. You think my writing's shit.

DANNY: What? No, Rose! I've read everything you've ever written. You're a wonderful writer.

ROSE: You haven't read everything I've ever written. You've read football scores and cyclone warnings. You haven't read what's in here. You fill these pages, Dad. Stories about you. Me watching you.

DANNY: I don't have any stories.

ROSE: So I give you a history that doesn't exist. I fill gaps. Taking bits here, bits there.

DANNY: Not very fair.

ROSE: It's all I've got. Unless you help me get it right.

DANNY: Oh, fucking hell. Leave it, Rose.

ROSE: I can't! I'm stuck with it. I'm carrying this huge black box around on my back and it's heavy and it's weighing me down and it's full of things I need to know but I'm not allowed to just put it down and open it! And that's why I ask you, Dad. Why I shove a recorder in your face, why I'm nosey. Because you're the only other person that knows what's in that box!

> BRIAN *enters.*

I'm your biggest war wound, Dad. I'm covered in your battle scars. I'm stuck in the middle of a war that ended <u>six years before I was even conceived</u>. That war is the only thing <u>I'm ever going to carry inside me, carry</u> on my back. So please don't tell me to shut up about it. I need to believe this never-ending fucking fight is worth it. Do you understand me, Dad? We're on the same side. Have some respect.

DANNY: Find your own life story, Rose. Stop feeding off mine.

ROSE: It's my story too, Dad. You passed it onto me.

BRIAN: All because you ran away from our fight, Danny. Tsk, tsk, tsk.

DANNY: It's finished.

> *Beat. She gets the pills out of her pocket.*

ROSE: Grandda… How much did you say Trevor sells these pills for?

BRIAN: Ten pound.

ROSE: And all these boxes need to be sold? The pills.

BRIAN: And phones. And cigarettes.

ROSE: And guns.

BRIAN: Oh, aye! And guns!

ROSE: Your boys make a killing, don't they?

BRIAN: They do. Audis. Overseas holidays. Big houses. Beautiful women.

ROSE: I'm looking for some new work.

DANNY: Rose. What are you doing?

ROSE: Shut up, Dad, this doesn't involve you.

BRIAN: We need a woman. Someone to bat her eyelids and wiggle her hips. Sweet talkin's so much more persuasive than some of the boys' techniques.

ROSE: I could sell these boxes.

BRIAN: I don't doubt it, Rose.

ROSE: You could teach me the business.

BRIAN: Everything you need to know, Rosey Maloney.

DANNY: Don't fuck around, Rose.

BRIAN: You could stay here with me till we get you fully integrated.

ROSE: I could stay here with you.

DANNY: I am not leaving you here with this man, Rose. Get your things.

ROSE: This is where I get my story, Dad.

BRIAN: One day, Dannyboy, you'll have to stop running away from fights.

DANNY: I've never been able to run away, Da. Rose, get your things.

BRIAN: You're a hollow man, Danny. All shell and no substance. You want to keep her as barren as you?

DANNY: Enough of this bullshit. Come on, Rose! Get your things.

BRIAN & ROSE: [*together*] She's/I'm staying.

DANNY: This man's the devil, Rose, do you know that?

ROSE: I want to meet your brothers.

DANNY: Fuck my brothers.

BRIAN: You have some respect for your brothers, Danny. They're good boys.

DANNY: They're not even here, Da!

BRIAN & ROSE: [*together*] *They'll be here soon!*

DANNY: I've just been on the phone to them all—they all forgot it was your birthday. They're not coming round. They're all busy.

BRIAN: 'Course they're busy. They work hard.

DANNY: Da, they're thieves! Thieves and drug dealers and thugs. Rich thugs. They're not hated because they're Irish Maloneys, they're hated because they're fucking evil bastards. And you want to become a part of that, Rose?

BRIAN: They're soldiers of the streets.

DANNY: Oh, Da. No one in your family's a soldier. They're all fucking runaways. Come on, Rose. You don't belong here.

ROSE: I do. I'm a Maloney.

BRIAN: [*to* DANNY] And you're a conscripted coward.

A long beat.

DANNY: Ask him about the IRA, Rose.

ROSE: What?

DANNY: Or the RIRA. Or the Continuity IRA.

BRIAN: The fuck are you talking about?

DANNY: Ask your grandda about the IRA, Rose. About his involvement in it.

BRIAN: She can ask me what she likes.

ROSE: He's already told me, anyway.

DANNY: Ask your grandda Brian about Mickey McKevitt.

ROSE: Dad, I don't know who you're talking about—

DANNY: Ask him, Rose. Ask this IRA soldier who Mickey McKevitt is.

BRIAN: Danny, I'm telling you—

DANNY: Ask him!

Beat. ROSE *turns to* BRIAN.

ROSE: Grandda, who is Mickey McKevitt?

BRIAN *says nothing.*

Granddad?

Nothing.

Grandda?

BRIAN: [*to* DANNY] I was testing you.

DANNY: Who is he then, Da?

BRIAN: How dare you.

DANNY: Who is he?

Nothing.

Who is he? Mickey McKevitt, Da.

BRIAN *stands firm, glaring. Says nothing.*

He's the leader of the Real IRA, Rose. Currently in jail for the Omagh bombings. Now, Rose, ask him when he smuggled that Semtex into the IRA meeting.

BRIAN: It was 1943.

DANNY: 1943. Well, that's interesting, isn't it, Rose, because it wasn't invented until 1966 and even then it was only the Viet Cong that were using it. Gaddafi didn't start selling it to the IRA until the 1970s.

BRIAN: Fuck Gaddafi. It was my own concoction. Looked just like Semtex ended up looking.

DANNY: Like sugar, Da?

BRIAN: Ay, like sugar. That's why I put it in a sugar bag, boy.

DANNY: Semtex is like plasticine, Da. It's like rubber. Nothing like sugar.

BRIAN: You little fucking bastard. You don't know anything.

DANNY: All those IRA meetings that kept you away from us all those years were just drunken nights at the pub, weren't they? All that money spent on the cause was really money spent at the bookie's, wasn't it, Da? I've spent the past thirty years trying to work out your soldier story and why it's so different to mine. Why you don't jump at fireworks and you don't have white turns and you can sleep and you can eat and you can talk about your fight until you're blue in the face and you can function at the age of eighty while I struggle to survive at the age of fifty-nine. And it's got nothing to do with the fucking Crown, Da. [*Beat.*] Guy Fawkes was in the English military, Da. So why the fuck have you got him propped up holding a can of Guinness? And Robin Hood is a fictional character. He's a story that's been added to and embellished by people who want to believe in some sort of hero. Some sort of martyr. [*To both of them*] Sound familiar? Brian Maloney and Guy Fawkes and Robin Hood and his merry men are all the same. You're all fiction and fantasy. You've never fought a battle in your life, old man.

BRIAN: And you have, you fucker? How dare you!

DANNY: I've fought. And so has Rose. And so has Glenys. We're the greatest fucking fighters in the world's longest-running war. And you're the enemy. 'Cause you fired the first shot with your lies and hatred. I won't have our fight swept under the carpet again by another fucking liar.

ROSE: Dad, calm down. Both of you—

BRIAN: I'm no liar. I'm a soldier.

DANNY: Liar!

BRIAN: You're the runt of my litter.

DANNY: Fucking liar!

ROSE: Dad—settle down…

BRIAN: Fucking coward, always running away. You deserve everything
you got.

>   ROSE *is stunned.* DANNY *starts to speak quietly.*

DANNY: By dark providence he was catched
>   With a dark lantern and burning match…

>   BRIAN *looks startled.*

ROSE: Dad…

DANNY: A penny loaf to feed the Pope.
>   A farthing o' cheese to choke him…

BRIAN: You know you're not to speak that verse, Danny.

ROSE: Dad, please don't…

DANNY: A pint of beer to rinse it down
>   A faggot of sticks to burn him…

BRIAN: Not in this house, boy.

DANNY: Burn him in a tub of tar
>   Burn him like a blazing star…

BRIAN: I'm warning you, runt, don't say it!

DANNY: Burn his body from his head
>   Then we'll say ol' Pope is dead.

>   *He rips Guy Fawkes' head from his body.*

ROSE: Dad!

>   DANNY *throws the dummy corpse at* ROSE *and she catches it,*
>   *horrified.*

BRIAN: You're poison spawn.

>   DANNY *goes to the boxes.*

DANNY: Which one's got the guns, Da? I'm going to put a bullet through
your brain.

ROSE: No, Dad—

BRIAN: You keep your hands off those boxes.

DANNY: Is it this one…? Or this one…?

BRIAN: I said keep your hands off those boxes, you fucking runt.

ROSE: Stop it, Grandda! You don't know what he's like!

BRIAN: You want a fight, Dannyboy? Is that it?

DANNY: Which box is it, Da? Which box, hollow man?

BRIAN: Don't you touch them, you fucking runt.

ROSE: Dad, please stop!

DANNY: I'm gonna kill you, Da. I'm gonna fucking kill you.

> DANNY *tears open a box, reciting the poem madly as he does so.*

> Hip-hip hoorah
> Hip-hip hoorah hoorah
> Hip-hip hoorah
> Hip-hip hoorah hoorah

> *Beat. He starts opening another one.*

> Hip-hip hoorah
> Hip-hip hoorah hoorah
> Hip-hip hoorah
> Hip-hip hoorah hoorah

> *Beat. Another box.*

> Hip-hip hoorah
> Hip-hip hoorah hoorah
> Hip-hip…

> *Beat.*

You sick bastard.

> DANNY *tips over the boxes. They are empty. He tears apart Guy Fawkes, searching.*

You cunt.

> *Beat.* ROSE *walks toward her grandfather. She takes his pills, gets one out and eats it.*

ROSE: Breath mint.

> BRIAN *leaps up from his chair and runs to the balloons hanging on the wall. He wraps the string around and around and around his neck and leans out from the wall until the string is taut.* ROSE *and* DANNY *do nothing. The string snaps and* BRIAN *falls in a heap. Beat.*

DANNY: So this is the way the world ends. You poor lying cunt.

He unravels BRIAN *'s pathetic noose and strokes his hair.*

I was so fucking lost, Rose. So fucking scared over there in Vietnam. But I told myself, this is the fight. This is the battle I should've stayed for in Notts. So just finish the fight and when it's over I can hold my head high and go home. But where was that, Rose? Where was that? In Australia I was a killer. And back here I was a coward. When I visited this family after the war I stayed just long enough to know I didn't belong before I laid down in Sherwood Forest and planted a seed in your mum's belly. Then I got back on that plane and tried to forget about it all. About that war. About this family. All of it. Then you came along. Another conscript. My little girl cut open and ripped apart and stitched back up and told it's no one's fault, be brave, shut up. So I obeyed my orders. Like a good soldier, I shut up. I don't speak about my story. People know my story. They do. They just choose to ignore it. But your story's new, Rose. I know that. I do, my daughter. And so I will help you. But not here. Not like this.

ROSE *nods, stunned.* DANNY *looks at his da.*

Come on, Rose. Let's go home. There's no story here.

The lights fade. As DANNY *and* ROSE *leave,* DANNY *gets caught on the barbed wire.*

♦ ♦ ♦ ♦ ♦

SCENE FIVE

DANNY *is again entangled in the barbed wire.*

ROSE: As we head back to shore, away from the murky deep and the dead dog, I watch my dad at the wheel. The wind whips tears up in his eyes, even though the boat doesn't seem to be going so fast anymore. As Dad rounds past a buoy, something knocks my foot. It's a cacker, left behind on the floor of the boat. As I lean down to pick it up, it snaps hard across my hand and slices a stain of blood into my palm. But I don't cry out. I just pick the crayfish up and throw it back into the water. Then I stand by my dad at the wheel and squint into the wind with him as we head home. As we wade through the water, he stumbles, and I hold out my hand to him. He takes it, but doesn't notice the blood on my palm.

DANNY *disentangles himself from the wire and moves slowly across the stage.* ROSE *watches him.*

As I help him to shore, I feel his own old scar against my new one. I squeeze his hand hard, and try to get it to go away. Squash his scar worm. Flatten it into skin, my own blood oozing through our fingers with the force.

DANNY *stops, trapped by the sight of his father, still on stage.*

But no matter how hard I try, no matter how hard I fight, I just can't seem to squish the little bastard scar. But that's okay. Because it just makes us hold on tighter.

ROSE *calls out to her father.*

Time to come home, hey, Dannyboy?

She holds out her hands and he takes them. They exit together.

Blackout.

THE END

Danny Adcock as Danny (background) and Kate Mulvany as Rose in the 2007 Mimmam production in Sydney. (Photo: Brett Boardman)